CABIN

FROM VERNACULAR TO CONTEMPORARY ARCHITECTURE

ALEJANDRO BAHAMÓN
ANNA VICENS

Schiffer Publishing Ltd
4880 Lower Valley Road • Atglen, PA 19310

Managing editor:
María Fernanda Canal

Editors:
Alejandro Bahamón
Anna Vicens Soler

First part texts:
Àgata Losantos

Project texts:
Maria Rosa Badia Gener

Research:
Alexandre Campello
Ana María Alvarez Gómez

Proofreading:
Martín Molinero
Agustina Luengo

Art direction:
Mídori

Graphic design:
Montse Montero, Soti Mas-Bagà

Production director:
Rafael Marfil

Production:
Manel Sánchez

Editorial project:
www.latinta.net

First edition: September 2008 © Parramón Press, Inc.
Translation by Omicrom Language Solutions, LLC.

Library of Congress Control Number: 2013932498

Type set in Formata/DIN-Regular

ISBN: 978-0-7643-4324-7
Printed in China

Schiffer Books are available at special discounts for bulk purchases for sales promotions or premiums. Special editions, including personalized covers, corporate imprints, and excerpts can be created in large quantities for special needs. For more information contact the publisher:

Published by Schiffer Publishing, Ltd.
4880 Lower Valley Road
Atglen, PA 19310
Phone: (610) 593-1777; **Fax:** (610) 593-2002
E-mail: Info@schifferbooks.com

For the largest selection of fine reference books on this and related subjects, please visit our website at
www.schifferbooks.com
We are always looking for people to write books on new and related subjects. If you have an idea for a book, please contact us at
proposals@schifferbooks.com

This book may be purchased from the publisher.
Please try your bookstore first.
You may write for a free catalog.

In Europe, Schiffer books are distributed by
Bushwood Books
6 Marksbury Ave.
Kew Gardens
Surrey TW9 4JF England
Phone: 44 (0) 20 8392 8585; **Fax:** 44 (0) 20 8392 9876
E-mail: info@bushwoodbooks.co.uk
Website: www.bushwoodbooks.co.uk

INTRODUCTION 4

VERNACULAR ARCHITECTURE AND THE NORTH AMERICAN CABIN 5

A TRANSATLANTIC CABIN 9
THE ADVANCE OF THE FRONTIER 11
THE CABIN AFTER THE END OF THE FRONTIER 13
LIFE ON THE FRONTIER 14
KEY ELEMENTS: LAND, MATERIALS, AND TOOLS 16
THE CABIN, STEP BY STEP 18
BEYOND THE BASIC CABIN 21
AUSTERITY, PRAGMATISM, AND HARD WORK 22

FROM VERNACULAR TO CONTEMPORARY ARCHITECTURE 24

Buro II bvba / Buro Interior bvba **BARN HOUSE** Roeselare, Belgium 26
Bakker & Blanc Architectes **BRAILLARD HOUSE** Chénens, Switzerland 34
El Dorado **WILLOUGHBY-DESIGN BARN** Weston, MO, United States 42
Felipe Assadi **CASA BUZETA** Maitencillo Sur, Chile 50
3RW Architects **GEIRANGER VIEWPOINT** Flydalsjuvet, Norway 58
Taylor_Smyth Architects **SUNSET CABIN** Lago Simcoe, ON, Canada 66
Vidal & Sant'Anna Arquitectura **BARULHO D' ÁGUA VILLA** Aldea Batista Alves, Rio de Janeiro, Brazil 74
Broadhurst Architects **SHACK AT HINKLE FARM** Upper Tract, WV, United States 82
Verdickt & Verdickt Architecten **GREENHOUSE** Asse, Belgium 90
Hertl Architekten **SEIDELDL HOUSE** Molln, Austria 98
Rok Klanjscek **NEBESA MOUNTAIN RETREAT** Livek, Kobarid, Slovenia 106
Jarmund Vigsnæs Architects **NORDMARKA CABIN** Nordmarka, Norway 114
Markus Wespi Jérôme de Meuron Architekten BSA **HOUSE IN FLAWIL** Flawil, Switzerland 122
EM2N **SKI CHALET** Cafrida, Flumserberg-Tannenheim, Switzerland 130

IMAGE AND PHOTO CREDITS. BIBLIOGRAPHY 140
WEBOGRAPHY 141
DIRECTORY 142

INTRODUCTION

Alejandro Bahamón

As a general rule, examples of vernacular architecture, being buildings without any discernable creator, spontaneous and in existence for hundreds of years, are well known by everyone. The log cabin, originally from North America, is undoubtedly one of the buildings which has been most widely reproduced around the world. It is the supreme simplification of the architectural concept of a house, something that any child can draw, and a traditional icon of mountain life. However, the most interesting aspect of this building, made from wooden logs which are stacked and fitted together, is found in its strong link to the formation of the culture of the United States. One could almost go as far as to say that this simple construction was a decisive factor in the colonization of North America, the expansion of its borders and in the creation of a shared culture, up to a point where, in some regards, it has become a banner of national identity. This book aims to pay tribute to an architectural form which, although found everywhere, has been studied little outside of the United States. The first part of this book consists of a journey back to the origins of the log cabin at the hands of the first European colonizers, and then moves on to document their adventure as they found their way across North American territory, taking this constantly evolving architectural legacy with them. It gives a clear analysis of the form, materials, and building process which is vitally important in the task of interpreting an architectural form that is as romantic as it is efficient and flexible. The second part puts forward a selection of recent projects, conceived of by architects and designers from all over the world, which exemplify the different interpretations of this iconic feature of North American culture and the enormous influence it exerts on the design of contemporary works.

VERNACULAR ARCHITECTURE AND THE NORTH AMERICAN CABIN

■ GEOGRAPHICAL AREAS WHERE THE NORTH AMERICAN CABIN IS FOUND

VERNACULAR ARCHITECTURE AND THE NORTH AMERICAN CABIN

Embedded in popular consciousness as the rustic dwelling of the pioneers of the frontier, the North American cabin is a unique example of vernacular architecture. The iconic log cabin perfectly fulfills the main principles of vernacular architecture: anonymity, economy, and efficiency. However, it demonstrates some particular details which give it special interest: it originates thousands of miles away from where it developed; its transmission is not so much intergenerational as the result of the example of community, and its development as a syncretic North American product is parallel to the appearance of a new culture, that of the United States.

Building with horizontal logs is one of the main types of vernacular architecture in wood, despite being one of the least studied globally. This lack of attention, however, does not apply to the United States, where the cabin, even if it only equates to a small proportion of the country's vernacular architecture, has been extensively analyzed. Wood was not used in domestic North American architecture until the arrival of the pioneers on the Mayflower in the seventeenth century. Nevertheless, these first English colonizers were not responsible for introducing the cabin to the American continent, as they were unaware of this technique. The log cabin was brought over by Scandinavian and German emigrants, meaning that all the characteristics of the North American cabin had already been present in European vernacular architecture. However, in the Old World, not one example can be found of a cabin that replicates the American model, as it developed as a unique and original typology in the acculturation process of the New World.

The log cabin has been a cornerstone in the history of the United States, specifically during the expansion of territory towards the west. Its existence is inseparable from the American way of life, which was forged by the French and Indian wars and by Independence, as it allowed for a lifestyle, totally different from that of the inhabitants of the East Coast, to be replicated all over the territory. The vernacular buildings of this type, built quickly and relatively easily, allowed thousands of families to embark on the journey to the west, safe in the knowledge that there would be woods everywhere along the way for the building their homes—without needing to carry materials on the long voyage. They need only take a few tools with them.

The log cabin of the O'Brien family in North Dakota, in the fall of 1923. The photo forms part of the Fred Hultstrand Collection.

The first log cabins were usually simple temporary one-story buildings, made of round rough-hewn logs. Later, if living conditions improved for pioneers who were settled or for the next generation, the same technique could be used to build a permanent, bigger, log house, with more sophisticated finishing.

Although the technique of building with horizontal logs was much more advanced than that used for the simple cabin, the tremendous iconic power of this type of vernacular building has become embedded in the imagination of the North American people as the log building par excellence. The fact that so many studies have been carried out on this building type is explained not just by its interest as a vernacular structure, but also because that from the middle of the nineteenth century, it became a symbol of the American frontier.

Already, back in the presidential campaign of 1840, the cabin was used as a propaganda tool to tip the balance in the favor of the candidate William Henry Harrison. Likewise, the linking of this typology with Abraham Lincoln, who was born and raised in various log cabins, with stories about slavery, such as the world famous novel *Uncle Tom's Cabin,* and with mythical characters, such as Daniel Boone, has led to the formation of a romantic and nostalgic image of the cabin. On the other hand, today, this building is still a symbol of North American physical and social mobility, of the pioneer's freedom and individualism, as well as the family solidarity necessary for frontier life. Made into a national institution, the cabin represents the enterprising man who lives an honest, simple life close to nature and who fights to overcome many setbacks.

The evocative power of the cabin explains its survival in the face of the rapid increase in sawmills all over the land, which allowed cheap houses to be built quickly with wooden frames. The cabin has seen a resurgence over the last 200 years, even if the most recent re-interpretations, based on pre-fab models, have retained little of the original spirit of the pioneer's shelter.

Left:
Wood cabin in Missouri, taken down and rebuilt with the same wooden logs from 100 years ago.

A TRANSATLANTIC CABIN

The vernacular typology of the log cabin has sprung up since pre-history in places far from each other all over the world which, as a rule, share the characteristics of having regions with thick woodland, often mountainous, and with low temperatures. Scandinavia, Russia, Eastern and Central Europe, the Black Sea, Tibet, and Japan are some of the areas where this building prevailed due to the harshness of the climate and abundance of wood.

The oldest remains of wooden constructions, found in Poland, go back to the eighth century BC. Since the Iron Age, the inhabitants of the conifer woods of present day Russia, Scandinavia, and Central Europe have used the single-room cabin built with assembled horizontal logs, a direct ancestor of the North American cabin.

In America, the arrival of immigrants, whose traditions favored wooden dwellings, was the starting point for the spread of the cabin as well as homes with a wooden frame structure. Both types were ideal for a population of exponential growth and a country whose resources of wood had not yet been exploited. The harshness of the climate on the frontier tipped the balance

The early nineteenth century cabin in which Abraham Lincoln was born is inside a Neo-classical mausoleum.

Center and right: Lithographs from the presidential campaign of William Henry Harrison which exalt the humble qualities of the candidate with the cabin and hard cider as his emblems.

Left:
1874 color lithograph of Daniel Boone fighting an Indian to protect his wife and child.

Right:
The cabin belonging to Lithuanian Roy Fure, in Alaska, shows the skill in the technique of the newly arrived immigrants from Europe at the beginning of the twentieth century..

in favor of the cabin and against the wooden frame structure as, even though it needs less material, it is more difficult to build and offers less protection against the cold and other dangers common to the surrounding wilderness.

The first North American cabins were built by the Finns and Swedes who settled in the Delaware River Valley from 1638. These pioneers initially used log cabins as a temporary shelter, as they lacked the sophistication of their European homes and represented a return to an older Scandinavian way of living: round, rough-hewn, simply assembled logs, ill-fitting doors and windows, temporary clay or wood chimneys covered by branches, earth, or planks. Nonetheless, their initial rudimentary design varied to incorporate improvements resulting from contact with other building traditions, including those of the German and Presbyterian Irish immigrants who began to settle in Pennsylvania in the early eighteenth century.

In this fashion, the various styles of European cabin amalgamated into a single accelerated development within the framework of the great melting pot of nationalities that the Hudson and Delaware River Valleys had become. This transformation of the cabin, less organized than that seen in its places of origin, was also a response to the frequent need to ignore their own culture in the interests of simplicity and low costs. The cost was not the only starting point for the cabin, as the Russians also decided to use it widely during their occupation of Alaska, which was called Russian America at that time. During

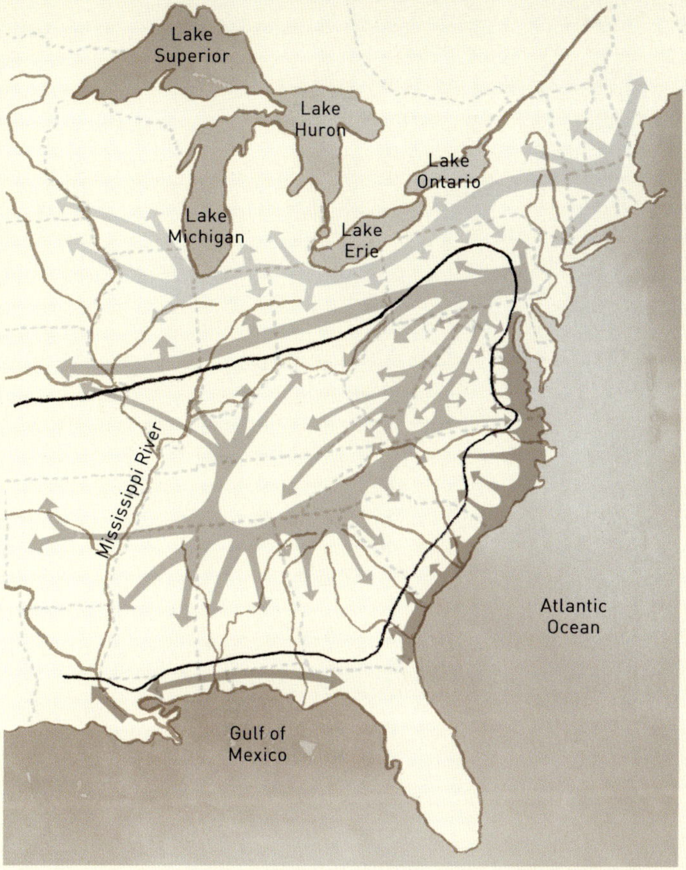

the eighteenth and nineteenth centuries, the Russians slowly settled on the Pacific coast and built a wide variety of trading posts, houses, and churches. The technique, generally more sophisticated than that of the pioneers of the east, used logs in the shape of prisms or cylinders to build houses of one or more rooms with one or more floors, and a roof made of metal sheets. The gold fever that took the new Americans coming from the south to Alaska in the nineteenth century meant the meeting of two building trends and the growth of log cabins in the region. The oldest city in the Yukon, Circle City, was the main exponent of this massive construction wave, as between 1895 and 1897 it was considered to be the largest city of log cabins in the world.

THE ADVANCE OF THE FRONTIER

The European pioneers spread quickly towards the Appalachian Mountains, which halted their advance until 1775, when the explorer Daniel Boone opened up a route across the forested Cumberland Gap. After the end of the French and Indian wars, which allowed for the crossing of the Mississippi in 1760, families ventured more to the west towards the Rocky Mountains, often in caravans in order to better defend themselves against Indian attacks. The United States' independence, awarded in 1783, added new regions to be explored, whilst in 1853, the year of the last annexations, the extension of the frontier was finalized. The expansion between Plymouth (East Coast) and the west of the Appalachians had taken 150 years; it took 50 more years for a considerable portion of the population to reach the Mississippi and,

Distribution of Building Methods

- New England trend
- Pennsylvania trend
- South Coast trend
- Area of the log cabin's predominance in 1850

Left: Cherokee Indians and their wood cabin, built on a reservation in North Carolina. The photo is by the ethnologist James Mooney.

Right: Cabin of a family of slaves on a cotton plantation in Alabama, in the south of the United States, in 1888.

finally, another half a century to colonize the two remaining thirds of the country. Shortly before the outbreak of the Civil War (1861), log structures had spread between New York and Florida, and as far to the west as the pioneer families had reached. This type of building was no longer just for isolated cabins in virgin territory, but now for building new frontier cities with schools, churches, barns, post offices, boarding houses, bars, tobacco drying barns, etc.

The process of occupying a new frontier territory usually followed the same pattern. When the family group arrived at the "promised land," they chose a plot of land, cut down the trees they needed and built the cabin that would serve as their first home. The hope of improving their living conditions drove the families to move towards the west, although they were all aware that prosperity was a long-term aim, and that life would be hard and lacking in comfort to begin with. The tradition of earning a living off a plot of land wrested from nature is the cornerstone of the pioneer folklore which has a very important place in the culture of the United States.

It should be added that the European pioneers were not the only ones to use the North American log cabin. The Native Americans, forced by white expansion to abandon nomadism and become sedentary as a consequence, also began to adopt this model of vernacular architecture from the eighteenth century. On the other hand, in the south the plantation slaves used this typology for the same reason as the whites: it was cheap and easy to build. During the hundred years that it took for expansion to go from the Appalachians to the Pacific Coast, the pioneers ceased to be European emigrants and became Americans. In these new settlements, the origin of the inhabitants was of little importance and it was usual for members of different cultures to get married. The ancestral ties were losing relevance for the new generations, who by then considered themselves Americans. This also had a notable effect on the configuration of the North American model of the log cabin as the direct relationship with ethnic groups or particular nationalities had disappeared. Lastly, the personal tastes and individual character of each builder prevailed, even if they were always restricted to the limitations of the environment and the materials available. During this period of acculturation which diluted cultural identities, the North American cabin emerged, a product of Scandinavian and German influences, but also of the modifications by the Presbyterian Irish and other groups. Once the frontier disappeared, there came a time when it was completely impossible to identify a cabin in terms of its nationality, as it had became a syncretic American product.

THE CABIN AFTER THE END OF THE FRONTIER

The proliferation of sawmills and the improvement of transport after the emergence of new settlements all over the territory brought about the peak of new building techniques which were quicker and cheaper than the cabin, such as wooden frames. Even so, the log cabin continued to be the first dwelling for many immigrants in isolated rural areas up until the beginning of the twentieth century.

The gradual disappearance of the cabin as a common dwelling coincided, at the end of the nineteenth century, with the emergence of a romantic movement which boosted its rebirth as a mythical image of a long-gone rustic way of life. The first signs of this resurgence appeared at the end of the 1880s in the Great Camps of the Adirondack Mountains, in New York State. These were camps made up of a series of buildings built of solid logs and designed by architects for leisure use by wealthy families. Inspired by the stories

Left:
Lake Forest Social Center, part of Lake Placid Club, on the banks of Mirror Lake in Adirondack Park (in the north of New York State).

Right:
Lodge keeper's cabin, Roosevelt Lodge, in Yellowstone National Park, in the central part of the United States.

of pioneers, such as Daniel Boone or Davy Crockett, these cabins were imitated in many resorts and leisure areas all over the country.

Decades later, during the Great Depression, the image of the cabin as a symbol of moral rectitude and civil pride was reflected in the plan to reduce unemployment by the Roosevelt administration, which got thousands of laborers involved in the construction of wood cabins, forest park ranger stations, watchtowers, etc., in the national parks. Much later, in the 1960s and 1970s, there was a revival of the movement which extolled a return to nature by self-sufficiency, and thanks to this, the cabin regained its previous prominence. Lastly, in the last few decades there has been a rise in the number of companies dedicated to building mass-produced log homes inspired by the style of the pioneer model.

Recently, it has been possible to see the noteworthy efforts that have been undertaken to preserve the log cabins of the eighteenth and nineteenth centuries through the setting up of pioneer museums nationwide. In fact, many North American towns preserve the original log structures of the first settlements, although they are hidden under the cladding of planks and plaster. It is not uncommon for the owners of a house to discover the honorable past of a building when carrying out home improvements, and the original log walls are uncovered.

LIFE ON THE FRONTIER

The United States frontier is a vague and flexible concept, as since the arrival of the first

Left:
The first building built in Dayton, Ohio, housed the Newcom Tavern. Nowadays it is in Van Cleve Park in the center of the city.

Right:
Built in 1930, the replica of Nashborough Fort in Nashville, Tennessee, highlights the structural techniques used by the pioneers.

pioneers, it has been steadily moved towards the west and the south until the unification of the territory in 1853. In 1690, almost seventy years after the founding of New Amsterdam (present-day New York), the consisted of only corresponded to New England, the banks of the Hudson and some scattered settlements in Virginia. At that time, anywhere that was out of the range of a musket ball was considered to be the frontier. The families went deep into the unknown with all their possessions, including animals, and, when they eventually stopped, they hurried to prepare their shelter: a log cabin. The first inhabitant of an area had to put up his cabin alone, or with the help of the family, but when a number of pioneers joined together the building of a cabin became a social act, the result of cooperation.

Given the great number of dangers that lay ahead on the frontier, the main priority when building a cabin was safety and defense. The sturdy log walls, without windows when things were very difficult, resisted the rustler's bullets and the arrows and attacks of the Indians. The first buildings were true fortresses, with roofs hardened with clay to offer protection from arrows and even underground hiding places to protect women and children. As the frontier was being inhabited, various groups of pioneers were able to get together to put up a fence with palisades around their cabins in order to increase their chances of surviving an attack.

The thick walls of the cabin were perfectly suited to the extreme frontier temperatures. If the corner joints had been carefully executed and the right sealing had been used on the logs, the robust walls provided interiors that were warmer in winder and cooler in summer. However, wood was not only used by the pioneers as a building material for their homes; they also made it a mainstay of their culture: stables, huts, barns, drying places, churches, courts, jails, and in a more domestic context, fences, furniture, tools, etc.

The frontier cabin was seldom thought of as a permanent building, but was rather considered to be, for the first stage of settlement, a temporary shelter where the family could live in relative safety and comfort until a sawmill could be opened in the area, which would allow them to obtain supplies of the material necessary to build a larger house. If the harvests went well, they were able to think about making the cabin bigger by putting extensions on the sides, adding another story or even building an annex onto the main building. On the other hand, if the awaited prosperity did not come, the families could choose to modernize their cabin by nailing planks to the outside of the logs eroded by the weather, enlarging the windows or doors, mending the roof with shakes, or covering the interior with planks or plaster. In many cases, after two or three years of exploiting the land, the family would sell and move further towards the west in the hope of improving their situation.

Life on the frontier made its mark on the character of the pioneers and, therefore, it shaped American culture. On the one hand the closeness of family bonds should be mentioned, as a hostile environment demanded the utmost effort from all members of the community. Each family was its own unit in terms of production and consumption, with tasks for all ages. Another cultural trait which came out of the pioneer era is the notable hospitality to strangers and new neighbors, a result of the need to create links with the community and guarantee mutual solidarity. Lastly, life on the frontier, which implied facing natural obstacles and cultivating self-sufficiency for survival, also gave rise to an individualistic entrepreneurial character and inventiveness to overcome challenges.

KEY ELEMENTS: LAND, MATERIALS, AND TOOLS

When building the cabin, the first factor that had to be considered was the location. The sun and wind usually determined the direction of the building. Sometimes it was preferable to have it facing towards the east to get the benefit of the morning sun, but due to the harshness of the climate, at times the shelter of the foot of a mountain was more suitable, whilst others chose to settle near streams or paths. A basic principle was that the cabin should have good exposure to the sun to avoid the logs rotting in heavy rain. Also, it was important to prepare the land by removing all traces

With wood being the main material for the house, it was the land and the experience of the builder that made a difference.

of roots of felled trees so that they did not affect the cabin's foundations over time.

Wood was an ideal material as, due to its flexibility and resistance, it responded well to compression and tension. These characteristics made wood the most suitable material not only for basic structures, but also for floors, stairs, panels, windows, doors, and furniture.

When choosing the trees with which to build the cabin, the builder had to look for smooth straight logs of a similar size, preferably old and without many knots. Ideally, the logs would dry out for a period of at least six months to prevent them from cracking, but in the case of the pioneers, who found themselves in a hurry to get a roof up under which to take shelter, this rule was often overlooked.

After choosing the trees, the builder felled them, cut them to the desired length for the cabin, and moved them to the chosen site. The logs could be used as they were cut, or sawed on two or four sides, according to the degree of sophistication of the cabin and the skill of the builder. Cutting them with a rectangular edge ensured a better fit, which eased the later task of filling in the gaps between the logs. Nonetheless, the most common logs found on the frontier were those that, due to lack of time and manpower, had not been planed down.

In general, a good size for a log was between 11.8 and 15.7 inches (30 and 40 cm) across and between 24.6 by 29.5 feet (7.5 by 9 m) long. The most popular species of tree were chestnut, oak, walnut, poplar, and fir, although the pioneers used the nearest type of wood they could find. Some builders avoided combining wood from different types of trees, whilst others used longer-lasting woods, such as oak, for the logs at the base, and softer ones, such as poplar, for the upper rows.

The axe, which was basically the only tool necessary for survival in the frontier territories, played an important part in the pioneers' daily tasks: cleaning the land, building cabins, making fences, gathering wood, etc. If this tool allowed them to build a basic home, then the use of other tools, such as a saw or a drill, enabled the finishing to be less crude.

The rocks which served as support for the cabin were used to level out the building, as well as keep termites at bay.

THE CABIN, STEP BY STEP

Most frontier cabins were built quickly: there are registers which hold records of three men cutting down the trees, moving them over to the plot of land, and putting up a one-room cabin with a chimney in two days. A person working alone would have needed between one and two weeks, but the cabin would always be small, as without help it was difficult to stack up more than six logs at a time. The plan of the cabins varied, but they usually started with a basic rectangle of 15.7 by 17.7 feet (4.8 by 5.4 m). The simplest had just one room; sometimes they were fortunate enough to have a window and included a loft.

Once the logs were ready, the foundations, if there were any, were laid. The technique varied in quality, material, and configuration according to the climate and the estimated length of time that the cabin would be used. The most common options were a continuous row of flat stones: piles of uncut stone masonry, small rocks, logs, sleepers or props directly leaning on a slope.

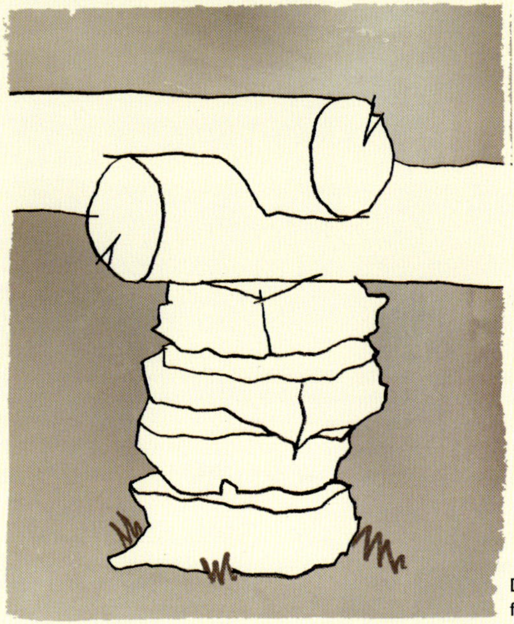

Detail of the foundations.

Except in the last case, the two props or supports were placed on the foundations, that is, the lower logs of the long sides which were usually heavier than the rest. The piled-up foundations helped to level the unevenness of the land and protected the house from termites and damp.

The shape and location of the chimney was the next step to be tackled, as it was commom to construct it first, before building the walls, and then fit the logs around it. Another option was to leave a space in the wall as it was being built to place the chimney in afterwards. The most rudimentary chimneys were built with clay and a light wooden structure although those that have been preserved until now are usually made of stone or brick. In more severe climates, they were put inside the house, but in the south they were usually built backed up against the out-

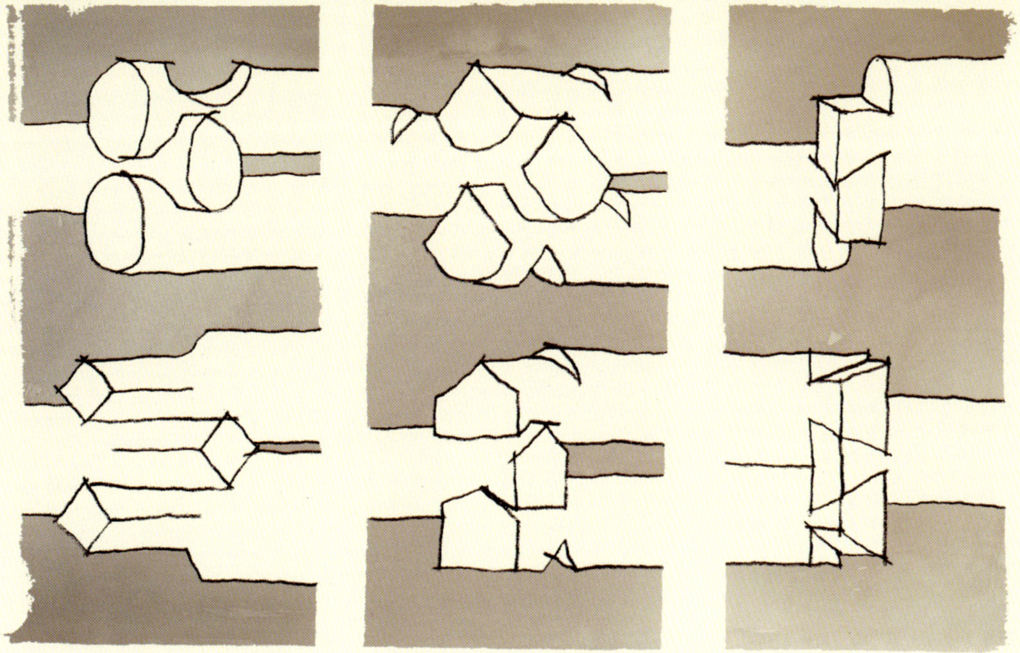

Details of the assembly.

side log wall. The location of those that were put inside varied: in the corner, at one of the ends of the ridge, or in the center.

The presence or absence of foundations governed the construction of the floor, which also varied according to the planned lifespan of the cabin. In the most precarious cases, the earth trodden down by footsteps acted as the floor, but it was usually made by laying planks on the framework of main beams and joists assembled on the sleepers. Some builders left the floor until the walls and roof were built to keep it from being destroyed by rain, which would slow down the building process.

After building the stone chimney, if it was decided to build that first, the walls, which were usually between six and eight horizontal logs high, were put up. The two longest, straightest logs, used as sleepers or props, were cut in such a way that the side leaning on the foundations was flat, thereby giving stability to the structure. The ends had to be positioned top to toe, that is, the base of the thicker of the logs, had to be opposite the upper end of the thinner log. This principle was also applied to the rest of the logs in order to achieve walls of the same height. The first logs with cut sides were assembled on the props and then the walls were built on top, by alternating the sides and fitting the logs in the corners to secure them. At around waist height, openings for the door and the windows were cut. The door was usually made from heavy planks of wood and the hinges from wood or animal skin. The windows, however, non-existent in the first cabins, were protected by animal skin or shutters made from planks of wood, and later on with paper, as glass

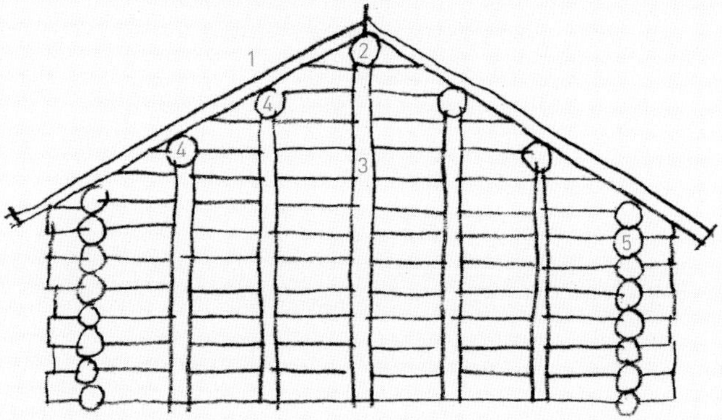

Purlin roof

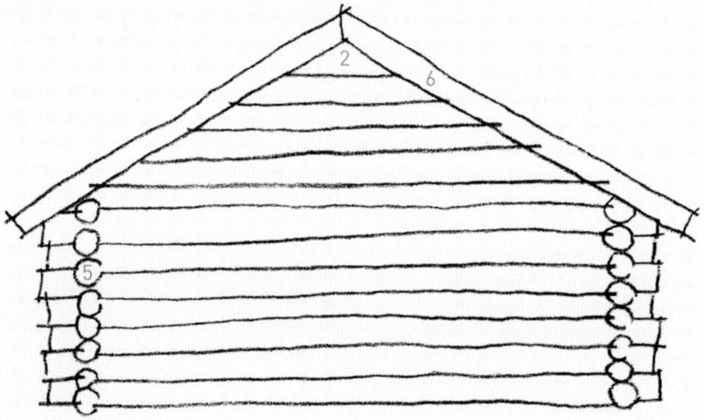

Rafter roof

Roof building
1 Rafter
2 Beam
3 Load bearing column
4 Purlins
5 End log
6 Rafter log

was not commonly used until the nineteenth century. The height of the upper part of the windows and doors was usually the same, and then further logs were added to finish the wall. Once the walls had been built, a loft could be constructed inside to provide extra space for sleeping and storage.

The angular fit of the logs provided stability and strength to the structure and meant that nails, or other securing methods, did not have to be used. This is one of the most characteristic features of this type of vernacular architecture. A great variety of techniques, with different degrees of flexibility, have been identified, from the simple oval or dome-shaped assembly, and the very common triangular version, to the sophisticated dovetail. The basic technique consisted of making a notch at the ends of the log, on either the upper or lower part, so that it fit perfectly to the log which was perpendicular to it. On the frontier, the different types of joints existed side by side depending on skill and taste, and the tools and materials available.

Depending on the precision of the fit of the assembly, the space between the logs could be very small, but usually after the walls were built and given time to dry, the cracks were filled to keep the building warm and protect it from insects and weather. During the time of the pioneers, the joints were first filled with pieces of wood and pebbles and then a mixture of hay and moss was applied on top and, lastly, a layer of clay. The results of this process were short-lived, and the filling usually had to be redone each season.

After the last log was placed over the door and window openings, the next task was to build the roof. Always gabled and with a slight slope, this is one of the most variable elements of the cabin due to the materials available. The most common structures were purlins (horizontal beams supported by the walls and distributed symmetrically between the ridge and the eaves) or rafters (joists placed perpendicular to the ridge). On to this frame the planks were placed that would then serve as a base for the roofing material,

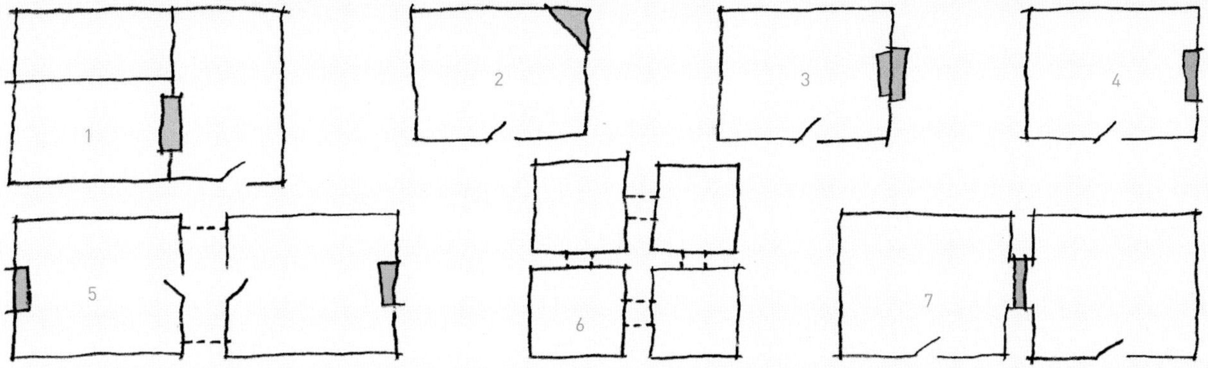

1 Central chimney
2 Corner chimney
3 Chimney on the outside of the gable
4 Chimney on the inside of the gable
5 Double cabin
6 Group of four
7 Shared chimney

Types of cabins

whether that was shakes, flat tiles, or other less elaborate systems such as branches, straw, or planks. A common method for raising the beams to the roof was leaning two logs diagonally onto the wall and using them as a ramp.

The finishes used on the cabin depended both on taste and the time available. The outside of the wall could be whitened with lime or covered with planks or plaster, often to show a change of status or to blend the outside of the initial building with an extension. Inside, the logs could be hewn or left unworked, and the cabins with better finishing were boarded with planks covered in plaster, paper, or cloth.

BEYOND THE BASIC CABIN

Starting with the basic rectangular cabin building (15.7 x 17.7 feet / 4.8 x 5.4 m), there were variations that could be made either in the shape or the finishing. On the one hand, internal divisions could be added or another cabin added. The most common types: the continental, consisting of a single building divided into three rooms organized around a central hearth; the double or saddlebag,

Right: The most commonly used model by the pioneer had two rooms separated by a central element (a chimney or a porch).

This building was part of the Tiptonville ranch and farm in the State of New Mexico. The picture is by photographer Donald W. Dickensheets.

made up of two parts together with a central shared chimney; and the dogtrot, two parts separated by an elongated breezeway – all under the same roof. On the other hand, contact with other cultures led the pioneers to use new materials, such as adobe, which was used to fill in the gaps between the logs in the buildings near Mexico.

AUSTERITY, PRAGMATISM, AND HARD WORK

Despite their austerity and small size, the shelter offered by the cabin was very welcome due to the plethora of dangers outside. In the worst cases, families, which were very large due to the need for manpower, had to share a single space of 822 square feet (25 m^2), tight quarters even if a loft for sleeping eased overcrowding. Because of the harshness of the winters in most of the country, the chimney was the central feature, both for cooking and for heating, until the appearance of the cheap kitchen in the mid-twentieth century. The interior fittings were usually simple and practical. The family would have emigrated from the east carrying all their most valuable possessions in a

wagon: plates, knives, clock, spinning wheel, candlesticks, bathtub, Bible, and tinder to start the fire. The man of the family used unvarnished wood to make the furniture: benches, chairs, beds, and a table. The lighting was meager and, if there were no candles, families used torches of loblolly pine or just the fireplace. The decoration was limited to firearms, hunting knives, or tools hung on the wall, although as time went by, the influence of Native American culture saw the addition of multi-colored fabrics typical of the Navajo and other tribes.

The worst discomfort was usually caused by insects, which came in through the gaps between the logs. As closed up as the joints were, over time the mixture began to crumble and the wind, rain, and snow ended up coming into the cabin. Also, if there were no effective windows, it was always too cold or too hot, and the air became stale due to lack of ventilation.

Despite these practical considerations, the cabin was the best option to meet the pioneer and his family's urgent need for shelter, without which it would have been difficult to venture into the country's unexplored forests. With a structure which was seemingly simple, but the result of extraordinary development and the combination of many cultural legacies, the North American cabin guaranteed freedom of movement for the pioneer. A handful of tools, a little knowledge, and almost no investment were enough for the head of any family to build a home in just a few days where it was possible to start a new life and, at the same time, contribute to the epic story of a country which would soon be dominated by cattle and fields of crops.

The interiors of the cabins were expressions of their inhabitants. It is in these spaces where the building technique is shown perfectly.

FROM VERNACULAR TO CONTEMPORARY ARCHITECTURE

MANY OF TODAY'S ARCHITECTS HAVE BEEN INSPIRED, CONSCIOUSLY OR SUBCONCIOUSLY, BY THE NORTH AMERICAN CABIN IN THE DESIGN OF SOME OF THEIR RECENT WORK. THE FOLLOWING PAGES GATHER TOGETHER A SELECTION OF PROJECTS, DESIGNED BY LOCAL ARCHITECTS, AS WELL AS CELEBRATED INTERNATIONAL FIGURES, WHO IN ONE WAY OR ANOTHER, REFLECT OR REINTERPRET CHARACTERISTICS OF THIS ANCIENT TYPE OF DWELLING.

The pictograms shown here are used for quick identification of the way the North American cabin has been interpreted; the new structure may have used the original shape, the building process or its material, or even a combination of these characteristics. Therefore, one or more of these pictograms are included at the beginning of each project with the aim of helping to identify the nature of each interpretation.

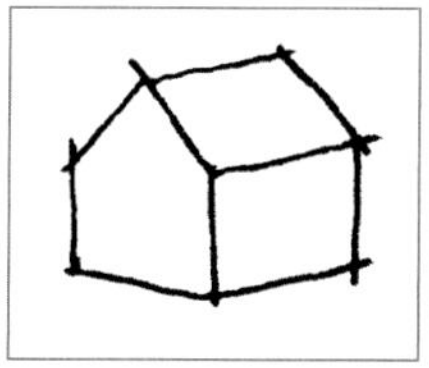

SHAPE A rectangular shape is the fastest and easiest way of building with logs of wood, whilst a gabled roof prevents the accumulation of water or snow.

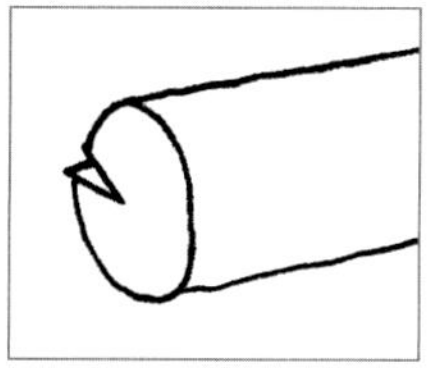

MATERIAL Wooden logs are flexible, durable, and plentiful in practically all of North America and easily transported and handled by a single worker.

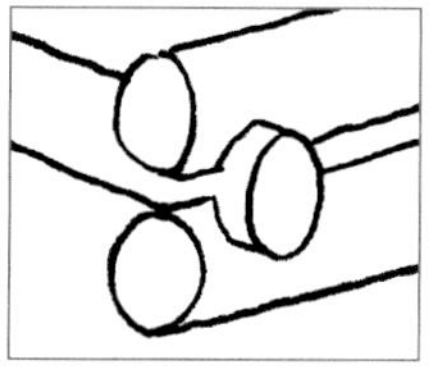

BUILDING PROCESS The placement of logs with notches on the corners allows for quick, highly efficient building, which is expandable and needs very few tools.

BARN HOUSE

AUTHOR BURO II bvba / BURO Interior bvba

LOCATION Roeselare, Belgium

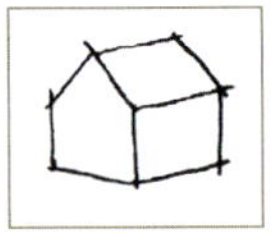 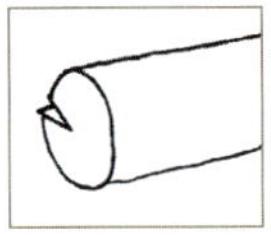

TYPE OF PROJECT House

SURFACE 1,017 feet^2 (310 m^2)

LENGTH OF CONSTRUCTION 12 months

YEAR OF COMPLETION 2005

PHOTOS © Kris Vandamme/Koen Vandamme

The Barn House is on the plain of Flanders, near the North Sea, in a rural, almost pastoral, setting. The architects of BURO II did not hesitate to take advantage of the opportunity to create a project inspired by the nearby hills and pastures. The house, therefore, represents an extension of the surrounding countryside. This modern cottage was built on the foundations of an abandoned farm.

Its design is positioned in the same direction as the original building and also imitates its shape. The rectangular-shaped floor forms an archetypal shape that is clean and simple. The gabled roof is covered by a uniform layer of wooden planks. Broadly speaking, the design is compact and it seems as if not a single ray of light penetrates the roof and enters the interior

of the house. However, the architects of BURO II widened the gaps between the shingles at the ends of the roof, where they form a kind of makeshift porch, on which light is subtly cast as it passes through. The furnishings and wall of the Barn House are a pure white, which contrasts with the dark slate floor: a modern and minimalist environment in the interior of a structure that alludes to the typical log shelter.

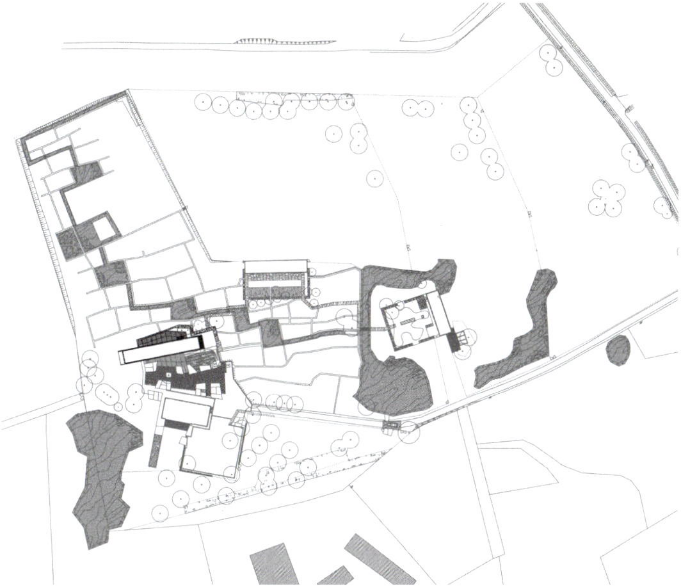

Site plan

The use of lumber and concrete as basic materials to create this building is no accident. Both materials are classics in terms of contemporary rural architecture. The footprint left by the barn that formerly occupied this space is key to the search for a synthesis between tradition and modernity. The inherent logic of the old dwelling is clearly shown in the exterior, whilst the interior is defined by a new identity.

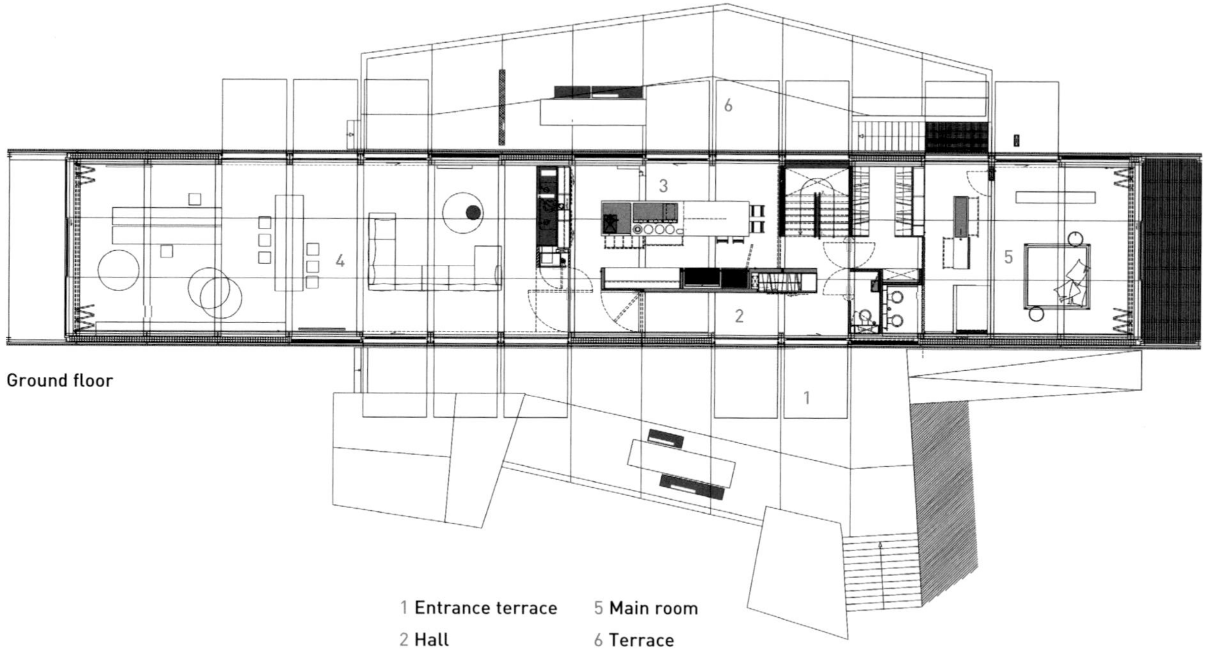

Ground floor

1 Entrance terrace
2 Hall
3 Kitchen
4 Lounge – dining room
5 Main room
6 Terrace
7 Bedrooms
8 Cupboard
9 Bathroom

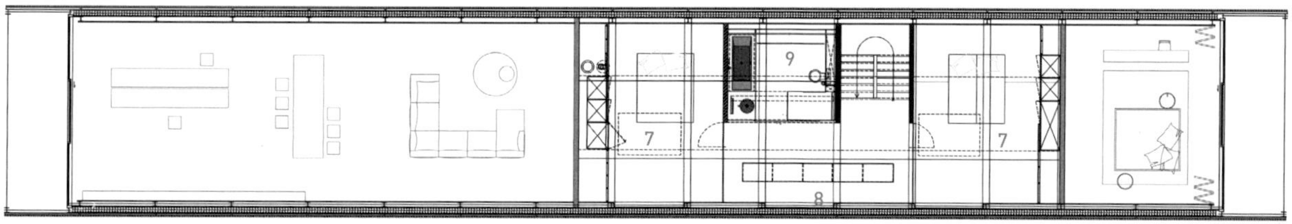

First floor

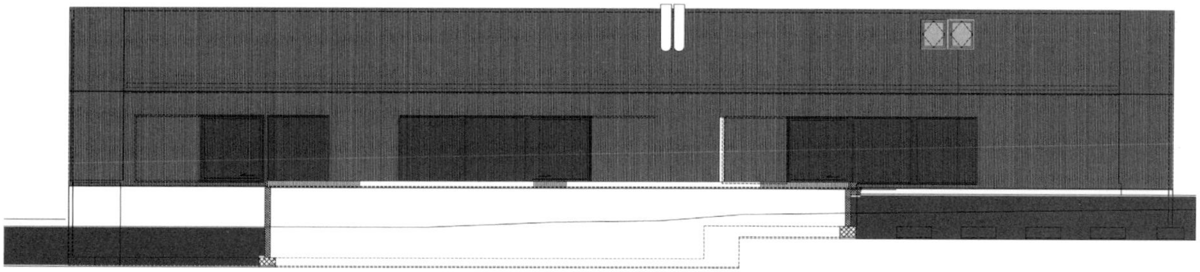

North elevation

The concrete structure allows for a clean and even interior, which recalls the barn above which the house was placed.

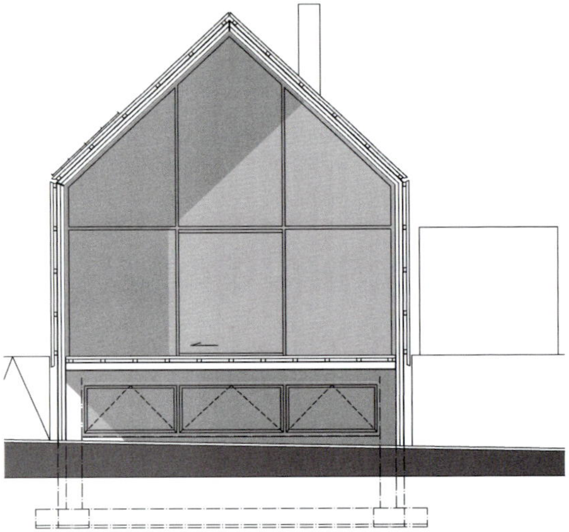

East elevation

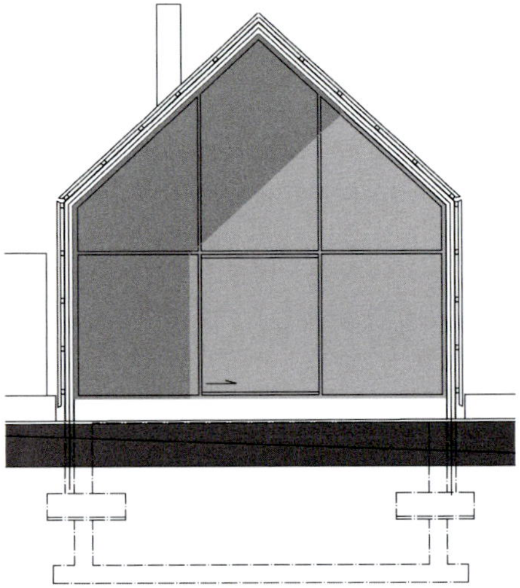

West elevation

BRAILLARD HOUSE

AUTHOR Bakker & Blanc Architectes
LOCATION Chénens, Switzerland

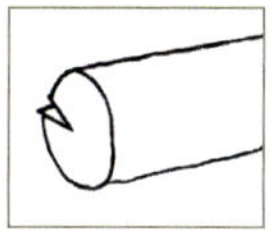

TYPE OF PROJECT House
SURFACE 623.3 feet^2 (190 m^2)
LENGTH OF CONSTRUCTION 11 months
YEAR OF COMPLETION 2006
PHOTOS © Marco Bakker

The Bakker & Blanc Architectes studio designed this house for a couple – young artists who wanted to live with their children in a rural environment. The house, on the outskirts of Chénens in the Swiss canton of Fribourg, had to meet the needs of the family as well as the work requirements of the clients. To do this, the architects created two separate areas which made a physical and psychological distinction between the home and the work areas.

Perfectly integrated into the surrounding countryside, the house is divided into two levels without any link between them. On the ground floor of the building there is the living area, in direct contact with the earth. For activities on a higher plane, such as creative work, the architects of Bakker & Blanc built a studio in the upper part, closer to the sky. The only connection between these levels is a small tube which they call a "talking tube," as only small objects the size of a teacup

can be passed through it. The mediation between the two areas is an exterior ramp, so there is no direct link between the levels; to enter from one world into another, you are forced to leave one world first to go outside and then enter into the other. Two concrete walls make up the base onto which a prefabricated building was placed. Although the materials are a long way from the traditional concept of the cabin – corrugated fiber cement, polyester and geo-textile – the

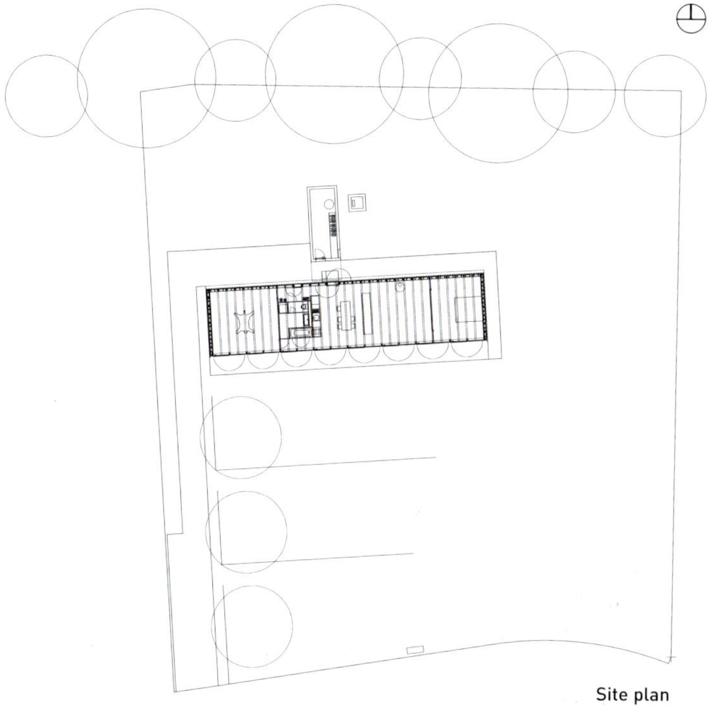

Site plan

overall effect blends in well with the rural surroundings.

The building method for the Braillard House, which begins from a pre-fabricated structure of wooden panels, meets the criteria for speed and practicality: two key elements in the building of log cabins in the past. And even though the legacy of this type of building is not shown clearly by the exterior, the desire to create a functional residence over time in a rural landscape remains unchanged.

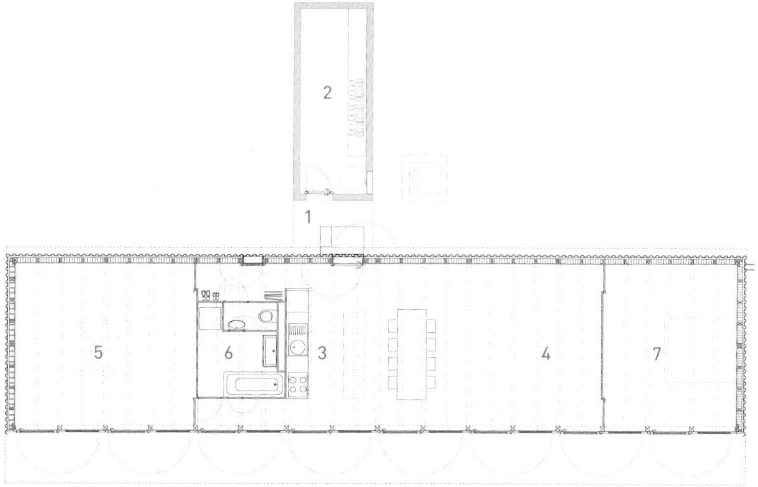

Ground floor

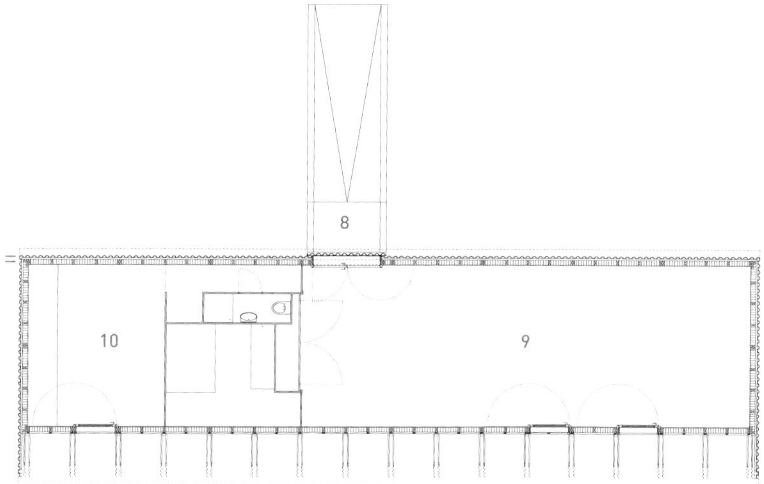

First floor

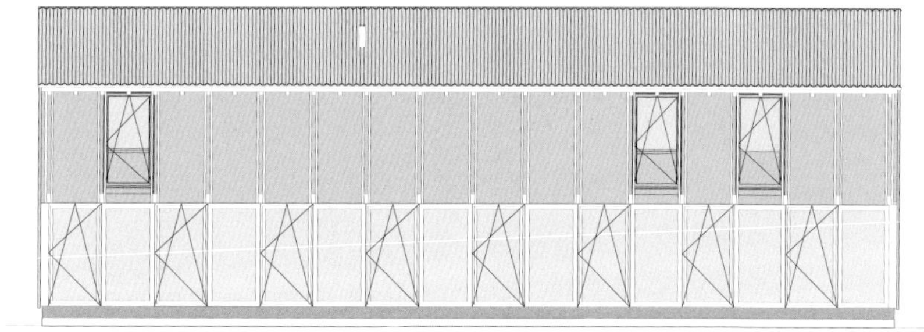

South elevation

1 Access to ground floor
2 Store room
3 Kitchen-diner
4 Lounge
5 Main bedroom
6 Bathroom
7 Bedroom
8 Access to first floor
9 Studio
10 Study

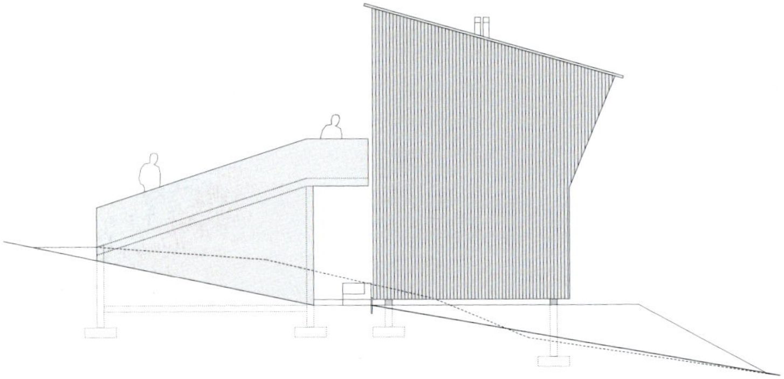

West elevation

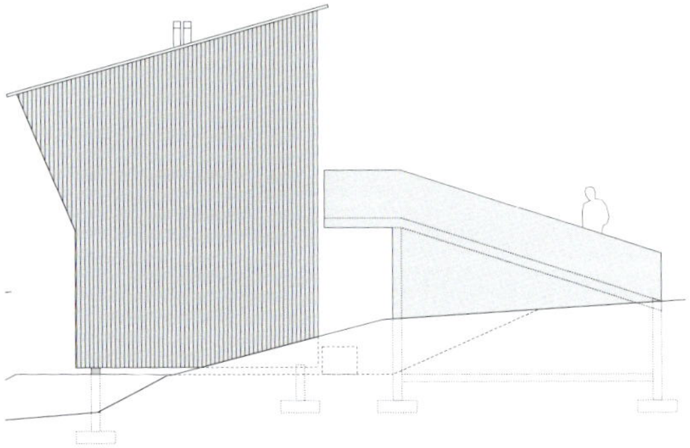

East elevation

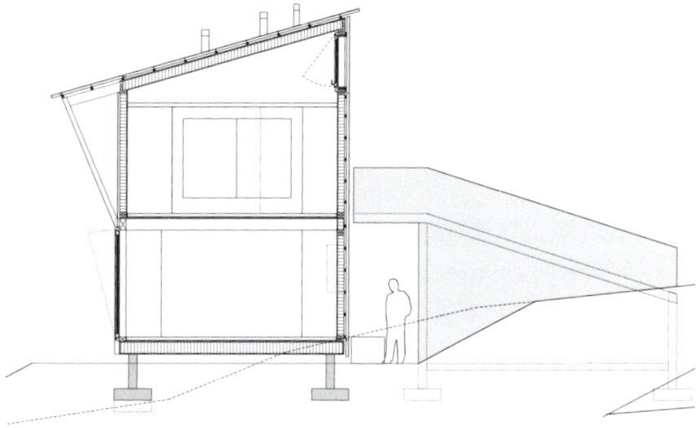

Cross section

INTERVIEW WITH BAKKER & BLANC ARCHITECTES

"THE PRACTICE OF "BUILDING THE BUILT" ALLOWS FOR THE APPEARANCE OF NEW FEATURES WHICH DO NOT CONFLICT WITH THE ARCHITECTURE OF THE PAST."

Which ideas inspired the Braillard House project?
The form of the house comes from local and traditional references, especially the features of the industrial and agricultural sectors and the traditional notions of "barn" and "farm."

How do you relate this project to the cabin?
The dual functions of the house, which come from the need to create an artist's studio and a house, are related to the isolation and self-sufficiency inherent in all cabins.

What can be learned from vernacular architecture and the cabin in particular?
"Building the built" hides a very well kept secret: a passion for the disappearance and the discovery of the extraordinary within the ordinary.

Why do you believe that the cabin has become an icon so closely linked to the home?
There is a kind of primary reflex in mankind that associate the "home" with "shelter." Together with the romantic desire to live free in dangerous surroundings, the cabin represents an oasis where it is possible to hide and feel safe.

WILLOUGHBY-DESIGN BARN

AUTHOR El Dorado

LOCATION Weston, MO, United States

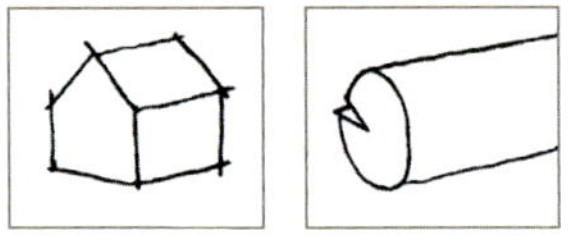

TYPE OF PROJECT Events pavilion

SURFACE 836.6 feet^2 (255 m^2)

LENGTH OF CONSTRUCTION 18 months

YEAR OF COMPLETION 2002

The Willoughby-Design Barn is an innovative space fitted out as an office next to a design studio in a barn originally built in 1880 in the suburbs of Kansas City, Missouri. Ann Willoughby put her trust in the architects of El Dorado to transform this barn into an innovative platform that would serve as a place to hold company events, together with the staff.

Apart from the industrial and agricultural functions, which took up part of the ground floor of the barn, the design of the space had to create a completely open space which would allow for various activities to be held comfortably, such as work presentations, small conferences, slide shows, and promotional events. The building designed by El Dorado meets all these demands: it has a

room which has been specially designed to meet these practical needs, and also has an independent area within the communal space, which is used as a relaxation room. The roof is made of corrugated copper and the panels are made of glass fiber. Thanks to the distribution of volume, visitors can enter the events room directly through two barn doors made out of cypress wood shingles. More than fifty

Site plan

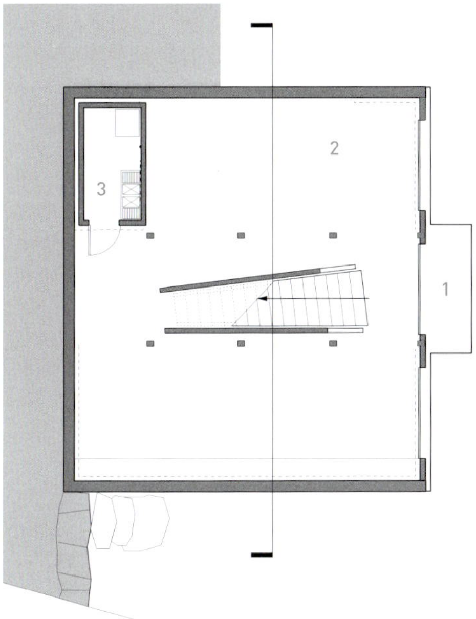

Ground floor

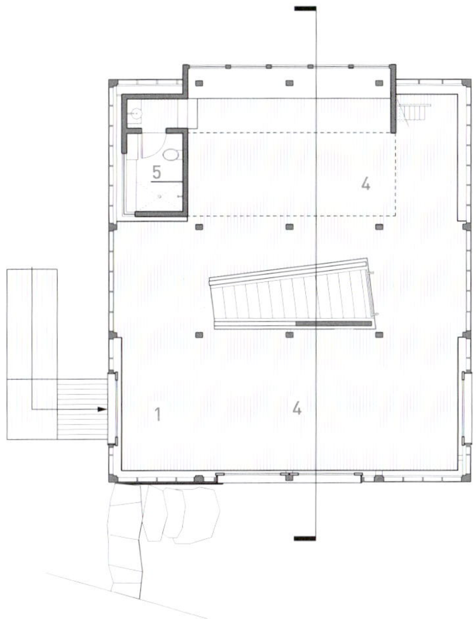

first floor

1 Entrance
2 Parking space
3 Store room
4 Events area
5 Bathroom

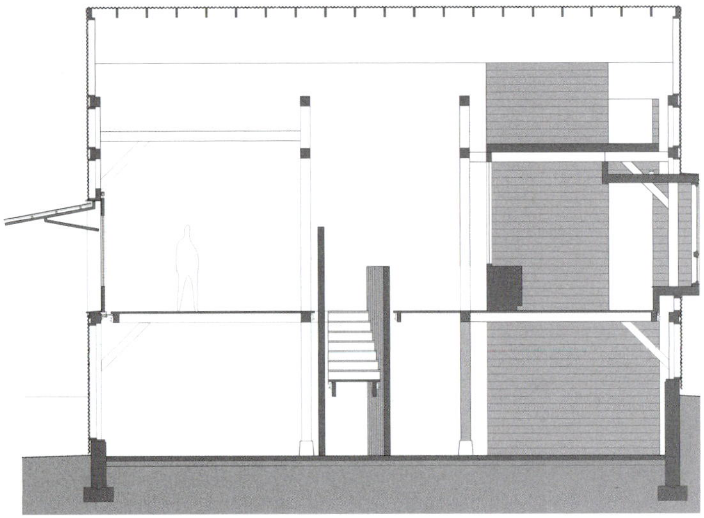

Cross Section

percent of the materials used in the restructuring of this space are elements which are reused or recycled. Other sustainable methods which were built into the space were an efficient cross ventilation system and correct positioning of the windows, which allow for maximum sunlight.

The Willoughby-Design Barn is a modernized version of a log house which keeps some of the intrinsic values of this type of building intact. The common work space, the simplicity of the decoration and the search for a direct relationship between man and nature as a source of inspiration are elements which are repeated in the traditional architectural model as well as its modern interpretation.

INTERVIEW WITH EL DORADO

“ CABIN MEANS SHELTER. OUR LIVES ARE COMPLEX AND COMPLICATED, WHICH IS WHY IT IS OFTEN PLEASANT TO EXPERIENCE SOMETHING SIMPLE ”

Which ideas inspired this project?
Despite the fact that the project was not directly inspired by the traditional wood cabin, it shares a certain likeness with another typology, the barn.

How do you relate vernacular architecture to your work?
The barn and the cabin are two typologies that offer basic solutions. Even if many of our projects do not rely on nostalgia as a form of expression, we are very attracted by the idea of preserving part of the openness of vernacular architecture. As we understand it, the barn is an example of a marriage between the vernacular form and modern expression.

What can be learned from vernacular architecture and, in particular, the cabin?
Often vernacular forms can give us guidance on the choice of a site and the details regarding weather conditions. They can also teach us to open our eyes and discover local materials which lead to the project ending up as an extension of the place where it is located.

CASA BUZETA

AUTHOR Felipe Assadi
LOCATION South Maitencillo, Chile

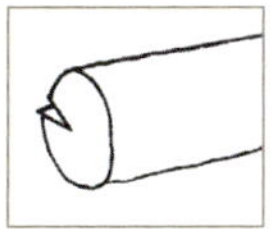

TYPE OF PROJECT House
SURFACE 367.4 feet^2 (112m^2)
LENGTH OF CONSTRUCTION 9 months
YEAR OF COMPLETION 2001
PHOTOS © Guy Wenborn

Casa Buzeta is a vacation home in South Maitencillo, Chile, located on a cliff that drops abruptly into the sea from 393.7 feet (120m) up, and has excellent conditions for paragliding. Felipe Assadi designed a shape which defies the wind and visually accentuates the pronounced slope of the site. The eastern facade of this building is completely transparent and made up of a double layer of wooden shingles that give weight and act as a kind of anchor to the daring building. On the side walls, there are two fish-eye windows which, together with the slope of the western face, outline the shape of a ship on the ocean's horizon. The interior of the house has a symmetrical layout and is presided over by a split-level space which hangs over the rest of the rooms.

The curvilinear roof of the building is inspired by the parachutes of the paragliders. The wide sheets of copper, which are evenly spread out across the roof from east to west, become wooden shingles at the part which looks out onto the sea, providing pleasant sporadic shade. The structure of the house is made from Monterey pine, the exterior from Oregon pine, and the roofs and chimney are made of copper.

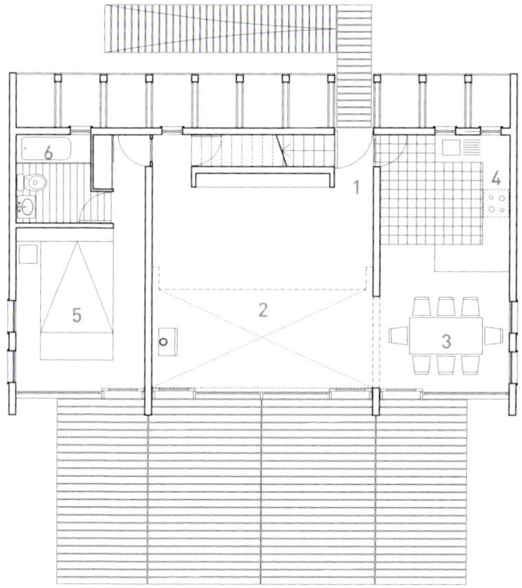

1 Entrance
2 Lounge
3 Dining room
4 Kitchen
5 Main bedroom
6 Bathrooms

Ground Floor

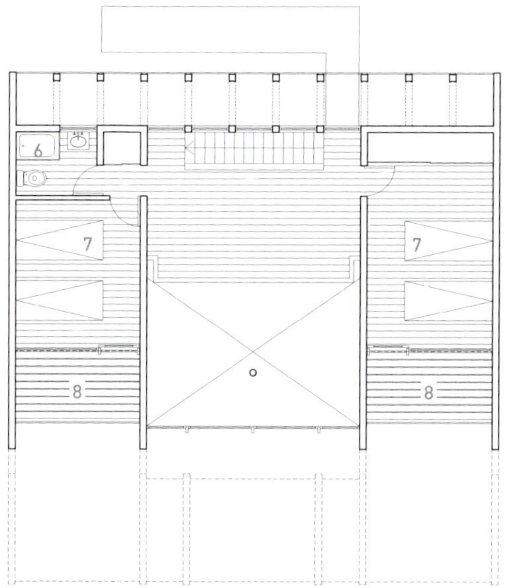

7 Bedrooms
8 Balconies

First floor

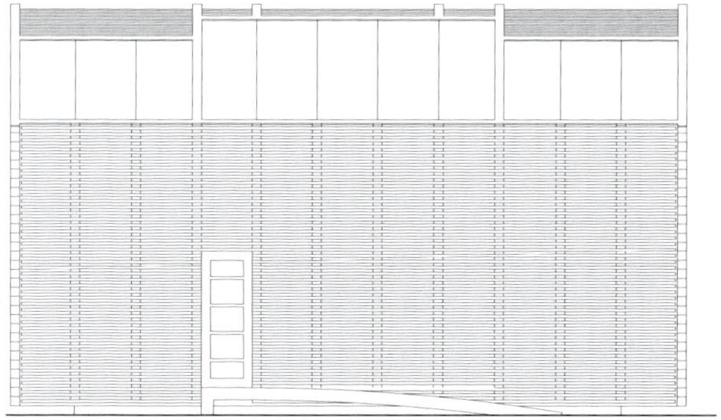

East elevation

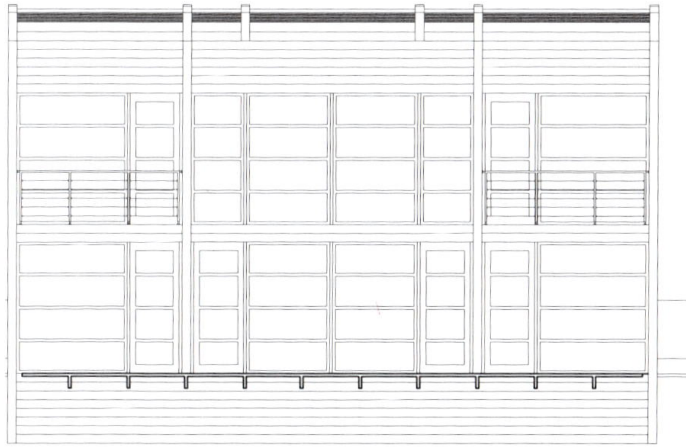

West elevation

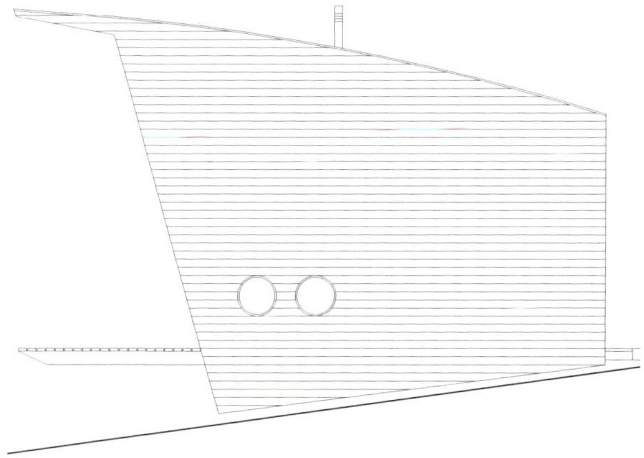

South elevation

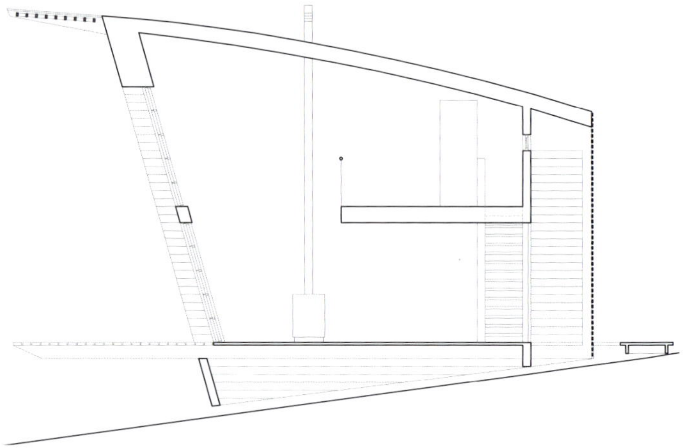

Cross section

Due to its robustness, wood has been one of the most commonly used materials for building houses, from the first European pioneer cabins to current times. Since time immemorial, the great iconic power of the log house has brought about ideals of freedom and conquering land, as the typical wood cabin is a quick and cheap shelter that can be built from a very simple structure. Looking out onto the immensity of the Pacific Ocean, Casa Buzeta stands with this same spirit of spontaneity and independence.

GEIRANGER VIEWPOINT

AUTHOR 3RW Architects
LOCATION Flydalsjuvet, Norway

TYPE OF PROJECT Urban facilities
SURFACE 557.7 feet^2 (170m^2)
LENGTH OF CONSTRUCTION 24 months
YEAR OF COMPLETION 2006
PHOTOS © 3RW Architects

The Geiranger Viewpoint is a very peaceful place where people can enjoy the view over the fjord of the same name, in the valley of Flydalsjuvet in Norway. The spot has recently been granted UNESCO (United Nations Educational, Scientific and Cultural Organization) world heritage status. During the period from May to September, the small village welcomes 600,000 visitors who come to take in the beauty of this spot.

The Norwegian authorities commissioned the young team from 3RW Architects to create various platforms from which to look out over the exceptional landscape of the fjord from different perspectives, outside structures to shelter the viewer, and multiple information points along the way. The project had to show off the beauty of the scenery and offer the growing number of visitors all the facilities to enable them to appreciate

the surroundings. It was also important to protect this remote place from the avalanche of visitors and therefore necessary to provide the area with the facilities needed to save it from destruction by the influx of tourists. Various lookouts have been placed on the steep slope of the mountain, along with parking and various buildings with services and facilities, connected by a walkway from which the landscape can be admired.

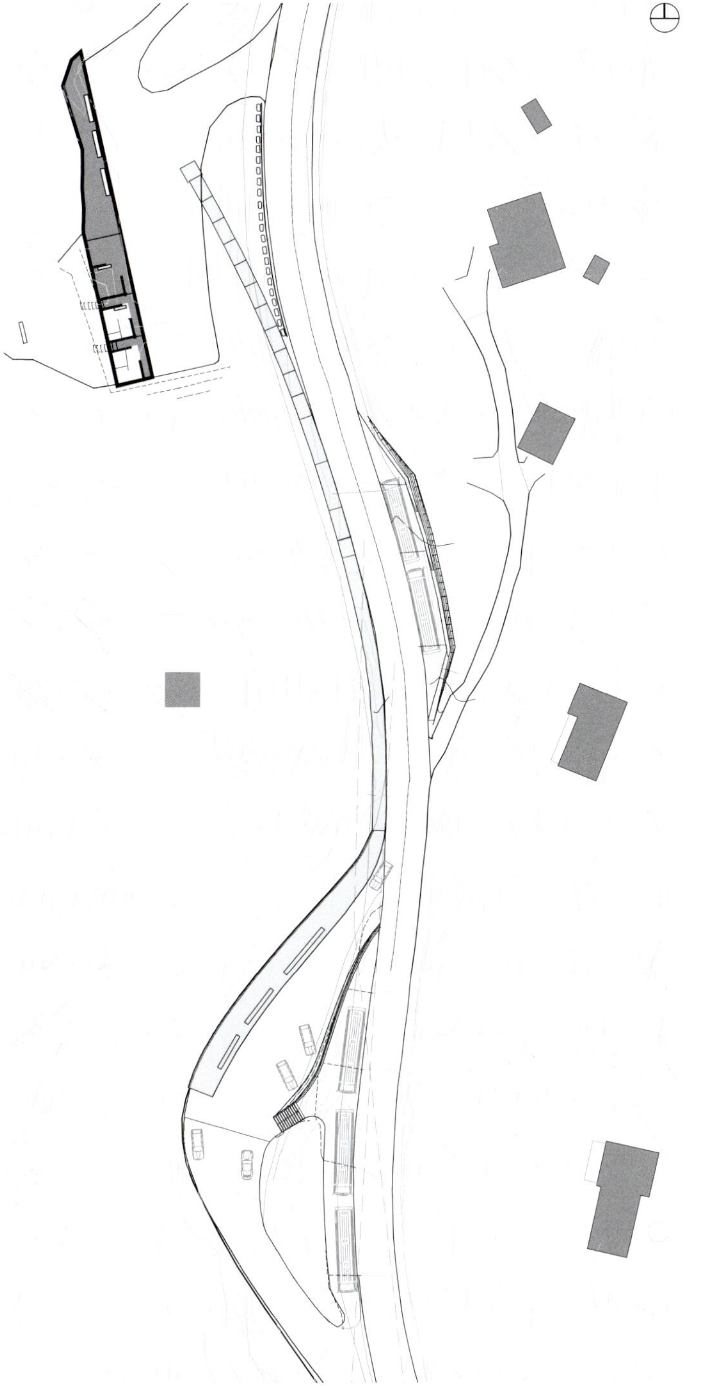

site plan

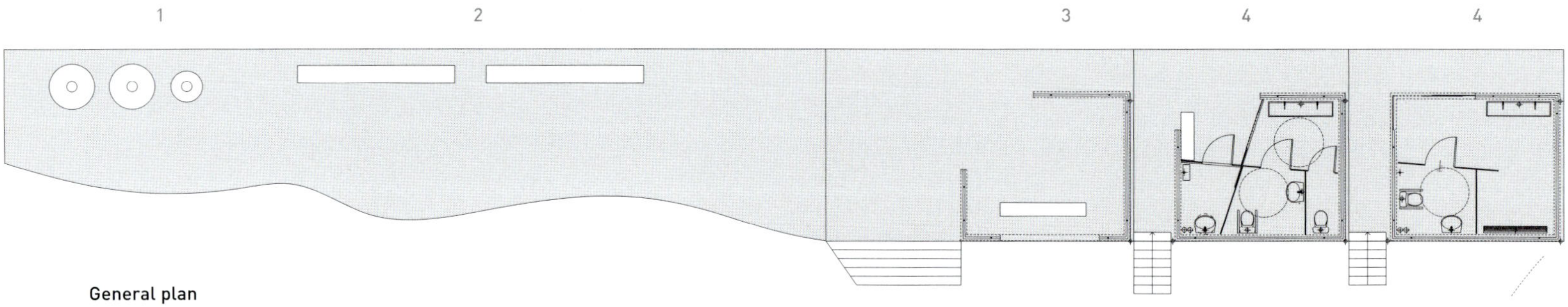

General plan

1 Recycling bins
2 Benches
3 Information
4 Washrooms

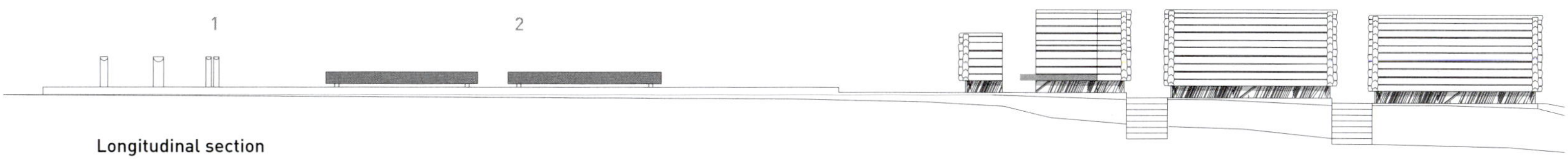

Longitudinal section

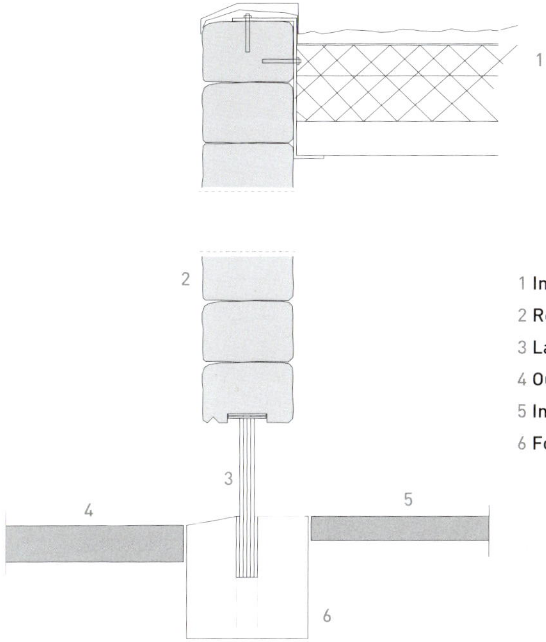

1 Insulating roof
2 Recycled wood
3 Laminated glass
4 Outside terrace
5 Inside space
6 Foundations

Construction detail cross section

The 3RW team recycled the logs from 100-year old authentic log houses and engaged specialist carpenters to fit them using traditional techniques, so that the new buildings preserved all the charm of the original structures. In this case, an old dilapidated barn was renovated by breaking it down into three pieces and moving it to its new site. To give more natural light to the robust log structure without altering the original facade of the house, the architects created a kind of glass base or square to allow sunlight to enter. One could say that this building transcends time: it preserves a traditional log house which is now floating on a modern glass base for the future.

SUNSET CABIN

AUTHOR Taylor_Smyth Architects
LOCATION Lake Simcoe, ON, Canada

TYPE OF PROJECT Cabin
SURFACE 76.2 feet^2 (23.25 m^2)
LENGTH OF CONSTRUCTION 1 month and 2 weeks
YEAR OF COMPLETION 2004
PHOTOS © Ben Rahn/A-Frame

This small romantic shelter, situated on the banks of Lake Simcoe in Canada, was created by Taylor_Smyth Architects, so that their clients could enjoy the beautiful sunsets in a single elegant space. The dwelling evokes all the romanticism of the old forest shelters of the Ontario area, built with the branches of the immense trees which grow in the country's forests.

The cabin consists of a wood and glass house located in a tranquil corner, separate from the main house which is right on the hill. The surface of the roof is covered by seeds and local vegetation to camouflage the cabin's visibility from the other house. The interior is reduced to a bare minimum: a bed with drawers, a wall with storage shelves, and a chimney for burning logs. It

seems that, when this small building was conceived of, it was assumed that a screen of wooden strips would hide the view of the lake. However, when looking at the screen closely, small gaps can be seen through which the landscape can be "spied on." On the west side, the strips gradually break up until they almost disappear on the northern most side of the wall, where there is a wide

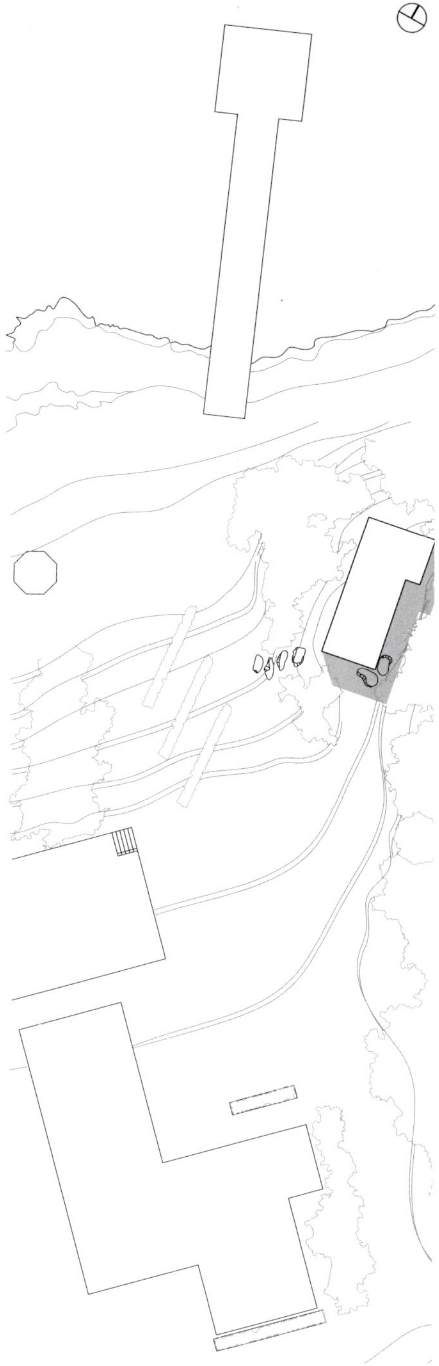

Site plan

and continuous lookout facing out towards the sunsets and the lake.

The variations in the landscape, due to the changes of the seasons, mean that the appearance of the cabin and the footprint it stamps on its surroundings vary from one season to another. In the winter, when a thick coat of snow covers the scene, the horizontal shingles of the building contrast with the vertical rhythm of the trees around it. In the spring, on the other hand, when the vegetation has grown new foliage and is in full splendor, the building is camouflaged by the green leaves. Regardless of the time of year, when night falls, the effect is always the same: a warm lamp which radiates its faint light out through the gaps in the wooden screen.

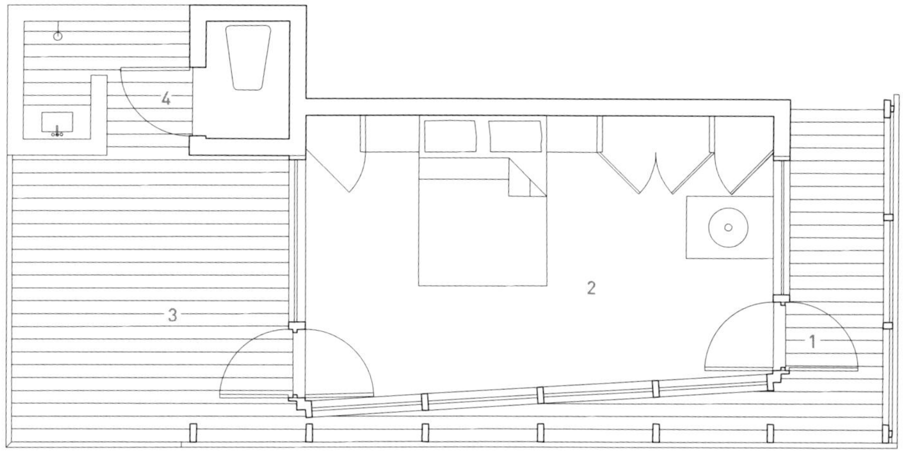

Plan

1 Entrance
2 Living area
3 Terrace
4 Washroom

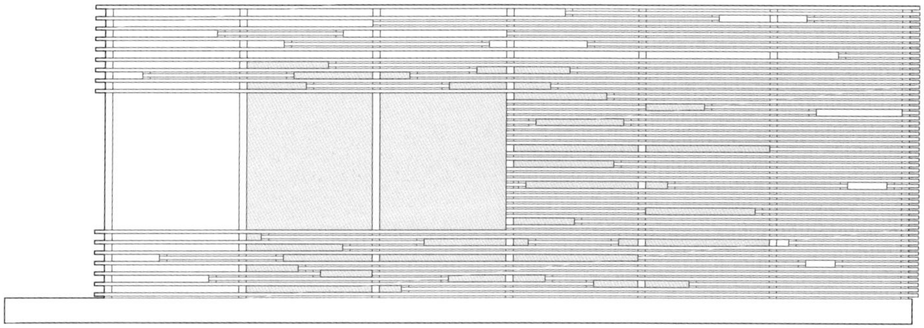

West elevation

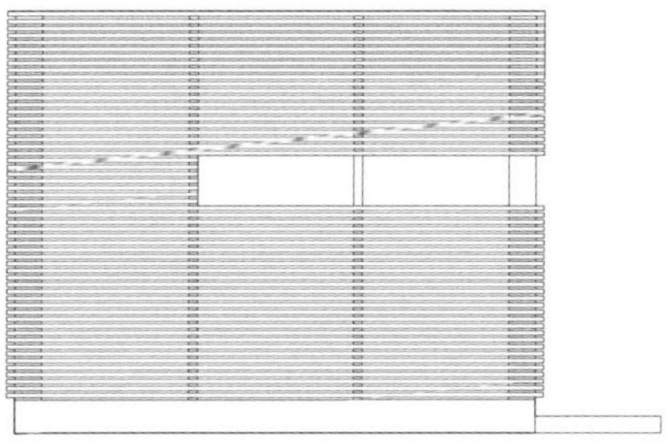

South elevation

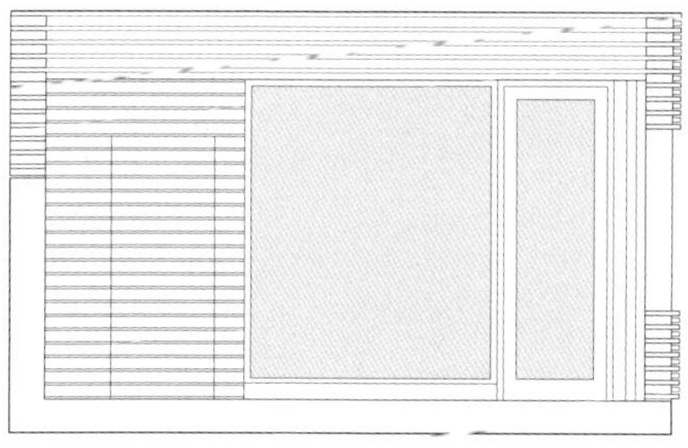

North elevation

The space between the wooden cladding and the glass wall acts as an air chamber which insulates the interior.

INTERVIEW WITH TAYLOR_SMYTH ARCHITECTS

> THE COLLECTIVE MEMORY RETAINS A RECOLLECTION OF A TIME WHEN PEOPLE WORKED COLLECTIVELY TO BUILD THEIR HOUSES.

Do you think that you were inspired in any way by the traditional cabin for this project?
Even if we were not consciously inspired by the design of the cabin, the analogy is relevant. For example, in terms of the appearance of the shape, we emphasized the natural gaps which give glimpses of the shingles to turn them into a characteristic feature of the project.

How do you relate vernacular architecture to your work?
We try to make good honest use of natural materials; however, the architectural language we use is important.

Why do you believe that the cabin has become an icon which is so closely linked to the home?
There is nostalgia in regards to this type of house and the first settlers. People relate to the authentic use of materials and the psychological connection between living in the forest and living in a structure made of the materials which make up the surroundings. There is an appreciation of artisan building and the idea of manual labor.

BARUHOL D' ÁGUA VILLA

AUTHOR Vidal & Sant'Anna Arquitetura

LOCATION Aldea Batista Alves, Rio de Janeiro, Brazil

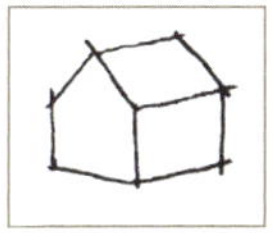 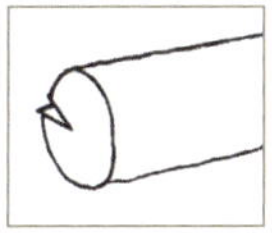

TYPE OF PROJECT House

SURFACE 492.1 feet^2 (150m^2)

LENGTH OF CONSTRUCTION 12 months

YEAR OF COMPLETION 2004

PHOTOS © Ary Condota

In a place which has been barely touched by people, 3.1 miles (5 km) from the city of Paraty, nature remains intact and shows off all of its splendor. The architects of Vidal & Sant'Anna had the opportunity to design a forest shelter in its purest form, showing respect for nature in an exercise of interaction with the tropical Brazilian rainforest.

The result of a careful study on the environmental impact of its construction, the building of this vacation house has managed not to upset the ecological balance of the environment with the presence of people. The house was built on an elevated wooden structure, the upper part is covered by clay tiles, and it has protective heat and sound insulation provided by large windows:

a transparent boundary which contributes to its complete integration into the landscape. The small number of elements which made up the Barulho d'Água Villa building meant that the building process was extremely simple. The use of modular structures and two large OSB (Oriented Strand Board) panels made the building of this house, done in stages, swift and simple. The problem

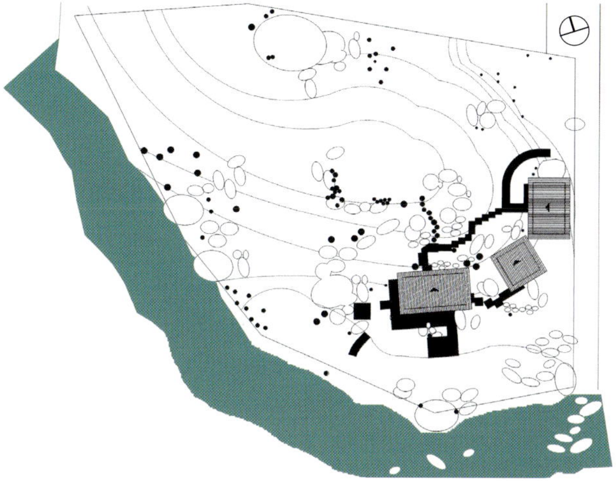

Site plan

caused by the natural unevenness of the ground on the site of the house was overcome by using separate modules, which fit together harmoniously with the main building. The large glass doors allow visitors to delight in a wonderful panoramic view of the lush landscape of the area.

The whole 492.1 feet^2 (150m^2) site is made up of various modules built between the trees and consists of a sensory experience that evokes traditional Brazilian cabins, as its design obeys the same aesthetic principles. The use of light materials, the efficiency of energy use, and the correct placement of the complex establishes a balanced relationship with all the elements of the area, at the same time achieving a cozy atmosphere inside the building. In this fashion, the project shows itself to be a sensitive solution to man's interaction in a delicate corner governed by nature.

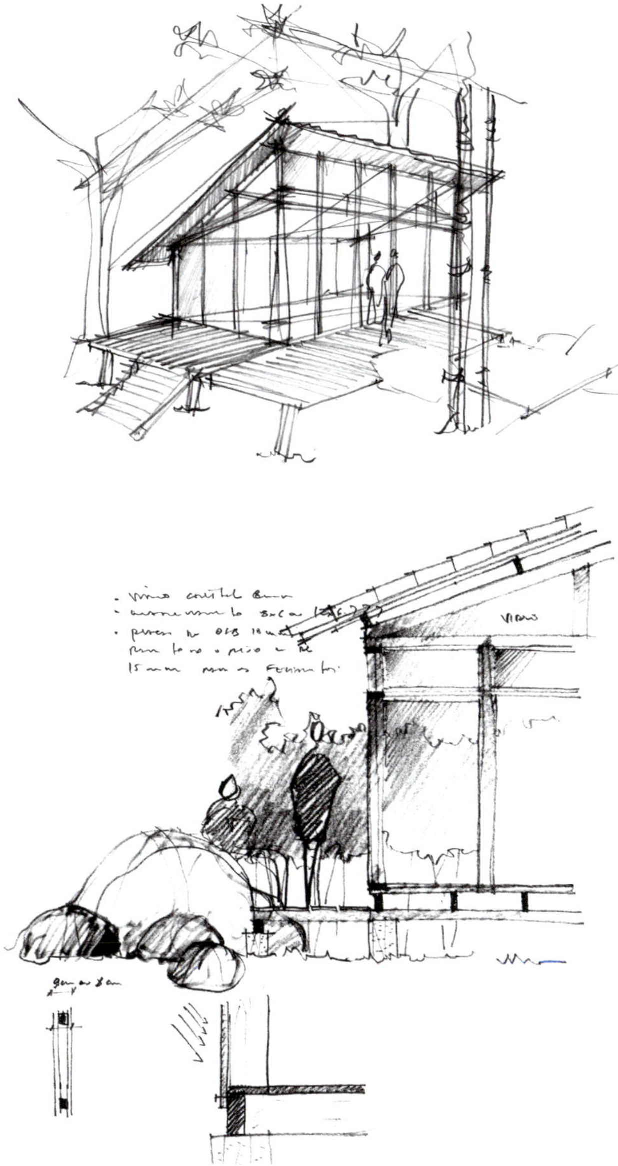

Preliminary sketches

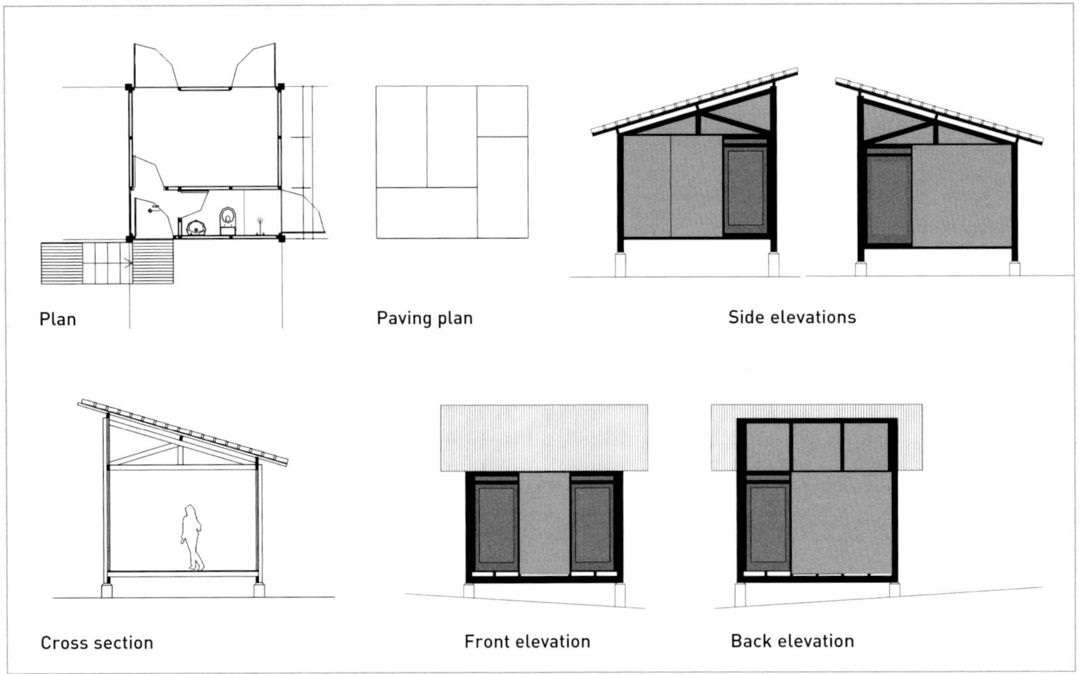

BEDROOM MODULE

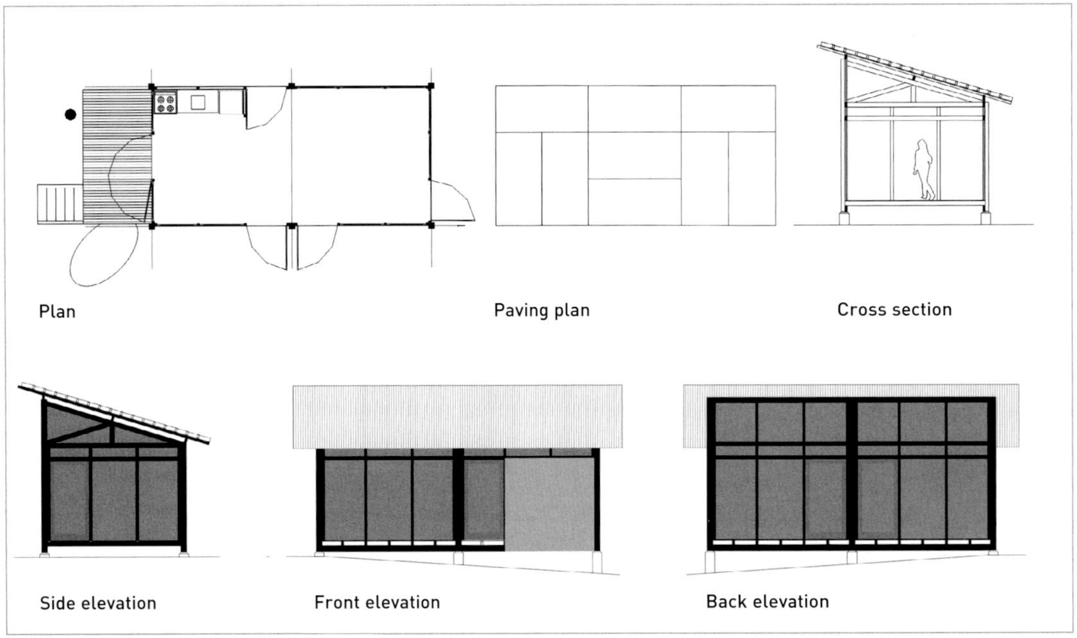

LOUNGE AND KITCHEN MODEL

> "THE USE OF NATURAL RESOURCES TO ACHIEVE BETTER SUSTAINABILITY IN ARCHITECTURE IS RESPONSIBLE FOR THE GROWTH AND ACCEPTANCE OF WOOD AS A BUILDING SOLUTION."

What inspired the Aldea Barulho d'Água project?
For this project, we thought about various elements shown by the building traditions of Brazilian vernacular architecture, such as the building conditions on the site. The access difficulties of the site influenced the cost of the project and the speed that we were able to execute it. Using that as a starting point, we looked for the ideal technology to carry out the project. The result of this search was a simple mimetic house.

What importance does vernacular architecture have in your work?
At its heart, this type of architecture has respect for the climatic, geomorphic, technological, and social characteristics of every site. By looking at vernacular architecture, we discover time-honored solutions. Our aim is to study the resources that come from this architecture with the admiration and sensitivity needed to understand them, adapt them and, as much as possible, even improve them.

What can we learn from vernacular architecture?
Contemporary architecture has the aim of a new building paradigm determined by sustainability. Some of the answers that we are seeking for this new paradigm can be learned through the typological solutions in vernacular architecture. For example, projections, orientation, local wind direction, and the choice of materials provide vernacular solutions that avoid the unnecessary energy cost of air conditioning, used in buildings with glass sides. Particularly in the case of the cabin, the use of wood as a structural or finishing material is another important example of vernacular techniques.

Why do you believe that the cabin has become an icon that is so closely linked to the vernacular house?
The recovery of the use of wood as a building solution has given rise to an aesthetic idea of establishing a differentiated language. This mainly occurs in houses where the sensory perceptions offered by the diversity of wood result in pleasant and inviting tactile sensations.

SHACK AT HINKLE FARM

AUTHOR Broadhurst Architects

LOCATION Upper Tract, WV, United States

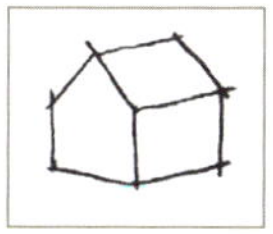

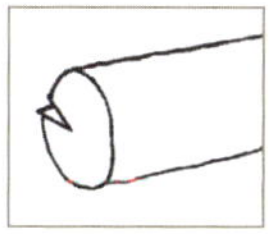

TYPE OF PROJECT Individual Cabin

SURFACE 60.7 feet^2 (18.5 m^2)

LENGTH OF CONSTRUCTION 48 days over 4.5 years

YEAR OF COMPLETION 2006

PHOTOS © Anice Hoachlander

This tiny rural cabin on South Fork Mountain, in the state of West Virginia, was designed by Broadhurst Architects as a weekend retreat for a family from the suburbs of Washington, D.C. In the vast terrain that is the site for this austere dwelling, there is also an abandoned farm and a cemetery, which give the countryside a hint of nostalgia.

As if it belonged to another era, the shack at Hinkle Farm has no electricity and uses rustic oil lamps to light the interior. The only source of heat comes from a small wood-burning stove, which is also used to heat water using a very simple hydraulic system. For the shower, there is a hand pump that is used to fill a water tank, installed above the user's head. The beginning of this sup-

ply system is outside the building, where the roof gutters collect the rainwater to provide for the family. The house sits on a platform raised up by four wooden posts, which help to prevent possible insect infestation. On the southeastern side, a porch opens out—protected by an aluminum and canvas canopy—which is accessed by a glass garage door. During the wet months, this terrace can

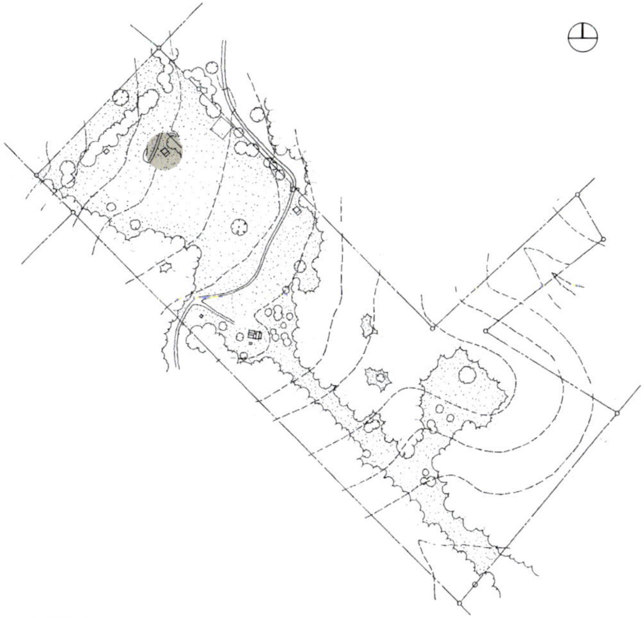

Site plan

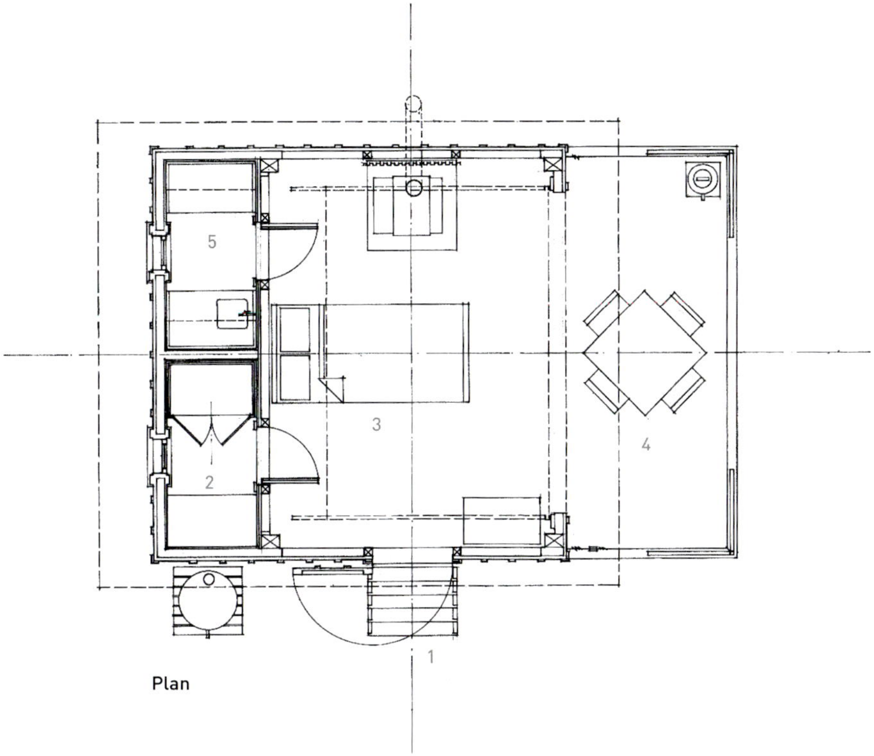

1 Entrance
2 Cupboard
3 Living-sleeping area
4 Dining room
5 Bathroom

Plan

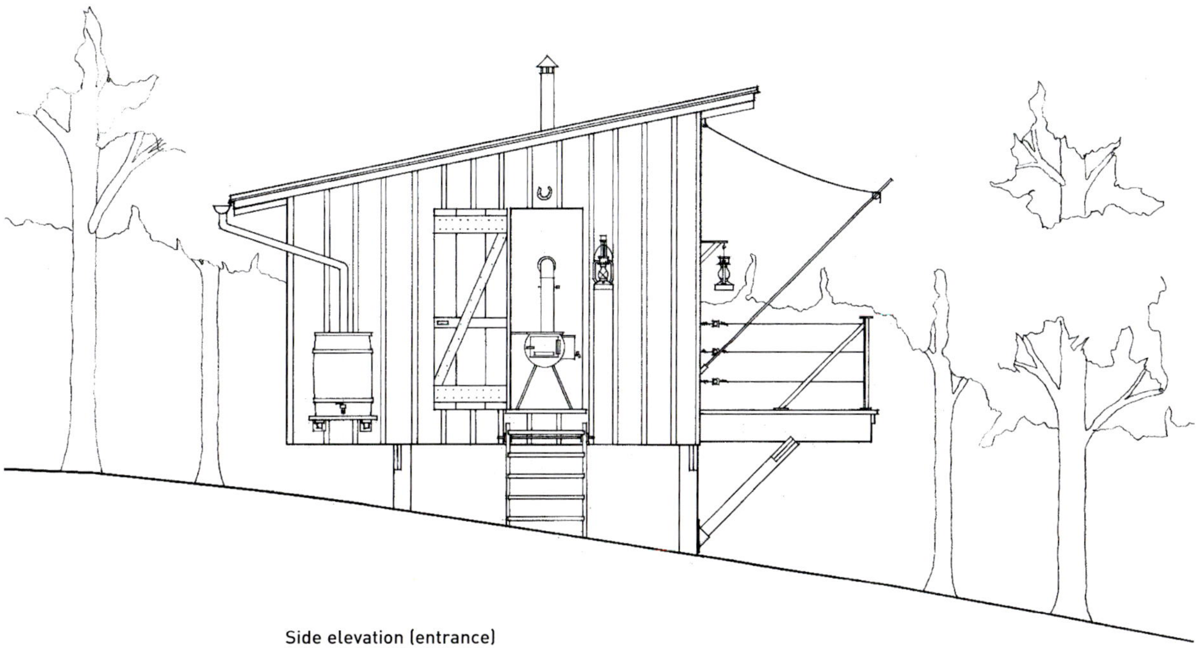

Side elevation (entrance)

be converted into an extension of the living space. On the northeastern side, there are small windows which allow the inside of the cabin to be ventilated with the pure mountain air, as well as provide the visitor with marvelous views of the grazing cattle in the nearby fields.

The Shack on Hinkle Farm seems to be frozen in time and is able to perfectly reflect the lifestyle of the era of traditional log cabins. The interior furnishing is so simple and practical that, in the middle of the twenty-first century, it transports the inhabitant of the cabin to the time when the austere American pioneers were moving towards the western frontiers.

INTERVIEW WITH JEFFREY BROADHURST

> HONESTY IS ALWAYS PRESENT IN THIS TYPE OF BUILDING.

How do you relate vernacular architecture and the cabin in particular, to your work?
Even though the project has certain similarities with traditional cabins, we were more directly inspired by the barns used to store corn and protect it from the weather and rodents. The building was designed to fit harmoniously into the surrounding countryside, using materials common to the local farms.

What importance does the observation of vernacular architecture have in your work?
Architecture is constructed from previous models and vernacular buildings are an essential part of this heritage. In the design of this type of basic construction, the practicalities and the details have to be worked out so they are honest and appropriate.

Why do you believe that the cabin has become an icon which is so closely linked to the home?
I think that we are all attracted to cozy, comfortable spaces with human dimensions that awaken a deep-rooted feeling in us.

GREENHOUSE

AUTHOR Verdickt & Verdickt Architecten

LOCATION Asse, Belgium

TYPE OF PROJECT House

SURFACE 679.1 $feet^2$ ($207m^2$)

LENGTH OF CONSTRUCTION 10 months

YEAR OF COMPLETION 2006

PHOTOS © Lander Loeckx

The enormous trees of the forested area of Asse, in Belgium, bear silent witnesses to the beautiful house designed by Verdickt & Verdickt Architecten. The greenhouse revises the classic concept of the forest cabin and offers some improvements to the vernacular model without diminishing its pragmatism.

This luminous and transparent building is sustained by a steel structure which supports a large glass door made of greenhouse glass. The outer shell forms a single continuous space over the various areas of the house. On the ground floor, there are the bedrooms and additional facilities. On the first floor, there are the study and lounge, from where the magnificent landscape can be appreciated. The walls are a combination of insulating glass and translucent polycar-

bonate plates. The reflection of the trees in these panels adds shadows which conceal the building. The house imitates the forest of ancient trees in a chameleon-like manner.

The design of Verdickt & Verdickt Architecten is an ingenious structure which provides simple, effective and practical solutions, such as the positioning of the house, which takes advantage of the sunlight or the

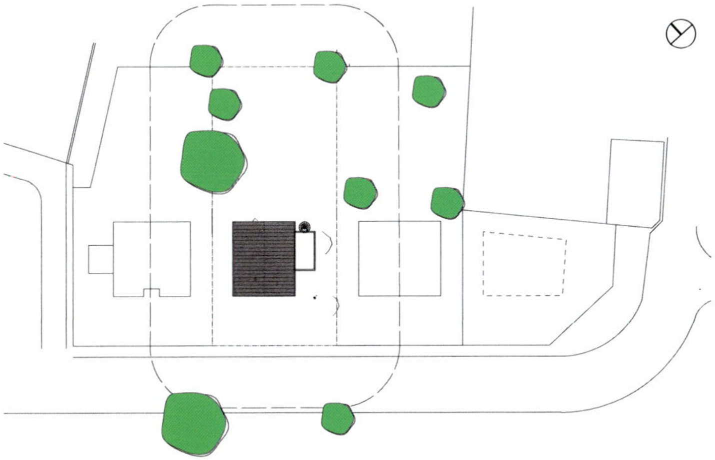

Site plan

intelligent use of energy resources in order to maximize energy saving by ecological and sustainable methods. This project offers a development of the typical wood cabin: with ingenuity and versatility, the maximum space has been achieved with the minimum amount of materials. The final result is a house which is sustainable and accessible.

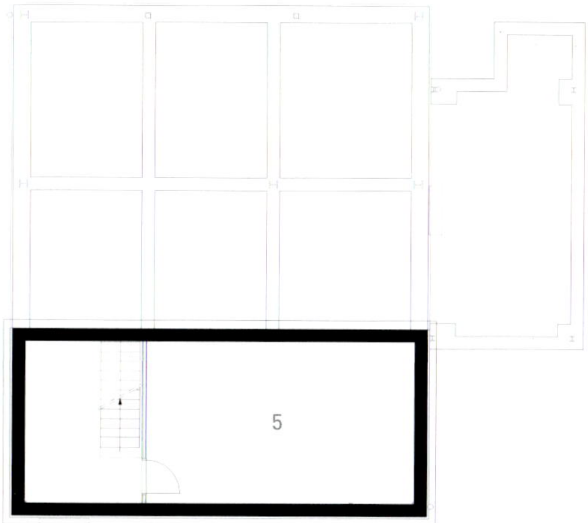

Basement plan

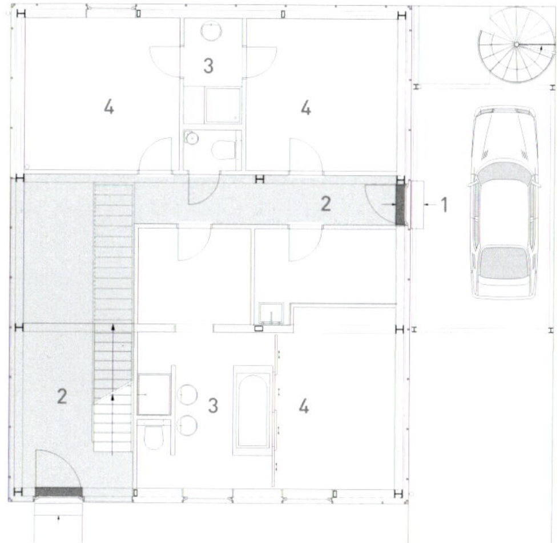

Ground floor plan

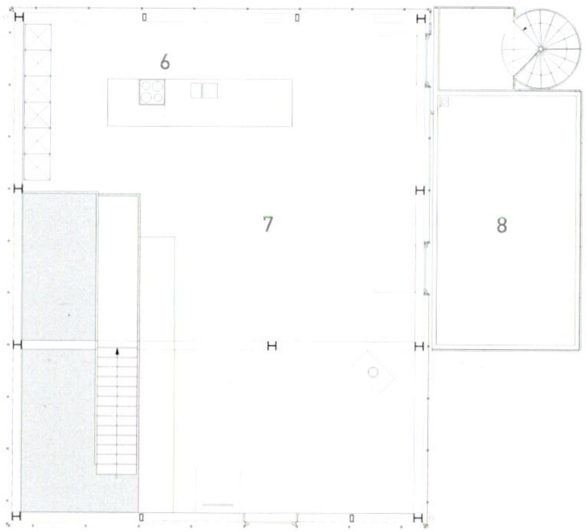

First floor plan

1 Parking space

2 Entrances

3 Bathrooms

4 Bedrooms

5 Store room

6 Kitchen

7 Lounge-dining room

8 Terrace

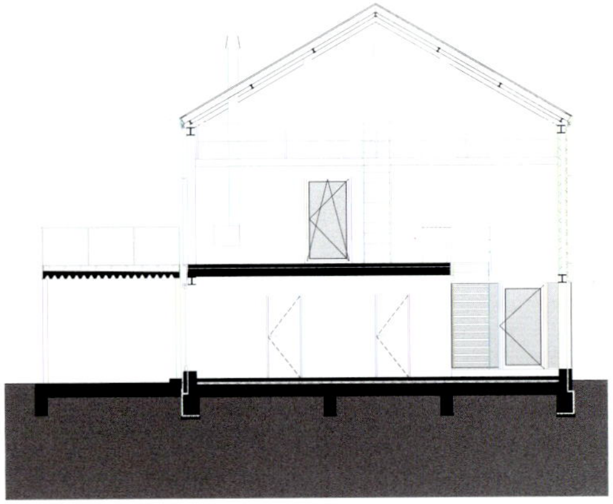

Cross section

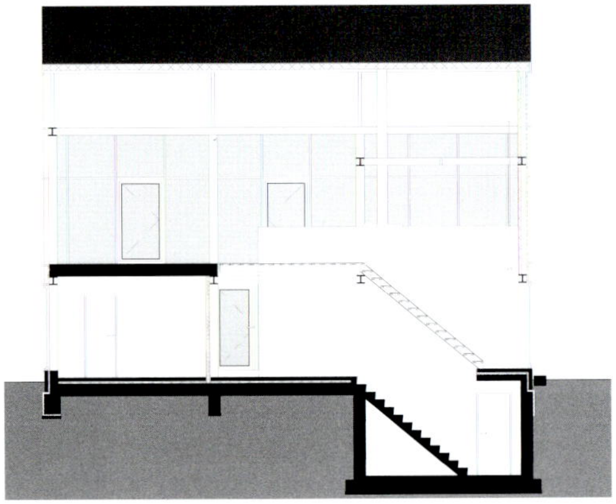

Longitudinal section

INTERVIEW WITH VERDICKT & VERKICKT ARCHITECTEN

"TRADITIONAL TYPOLOGIES FORM A STARTING POINT FOR A CONTEMPORARY AND LONG-LASTING IDEA; TRADITION IS THE BASIS FOR RENEWAL."

What was the starting point for designing the greenhouse?
The starting point for this house was the desire to develop a new type of house with an accessible price which was within the parameters of traditional building.

The result of this search was a house that was built with the minimum amount of material possible, which took full advantage of the inside space. Thanks to the building of this particular kind of facade, we created a space with a great capacity for insulation and capturing light.

What importance does the observation of vernacular architecture have in your work?
For us, architecture is a search for the "origin," the most fundamental. The essence of our projects is not to provoke, but to search for what is essential in order to create a clear and pure concept. As is the case with vernacular architecture, we try not to do unnecessary things so the final solution of the design becomes the most obvious. During this process, working with an approach that is rather unconventional becomes a means and not an end.

What can be learned from vernacular architecture and, the cabin, in particular?
Vernacular architecture has been considered to be the most rational and simple of typologies as well as the most ingenious. We are convinced that architecture should develop more often from this type of approach. A good example is the issue of durable buildings. Special techniques and materials have been used to make buildings that are less perishable, without considering the importance of correct orientation. Before, when a barn needed shade, a tree was planted, whilst today we dedicate ourselves to installing refrigeration systems which work day and night.

Why do you believe that the cabin has become such a cherished icon?
Superfluous details have been eliminated from the outside appearance of the wood cabin: this has limited itself to perfectly meeting the basic need of protection, that is, the essence of architecture. Also, due to its practicality, this typology has the capacity to adapt to necessary changes.

SEIDL HOUSE

AUTHOR Hertl Architekten

LOCATION Molln, Austria

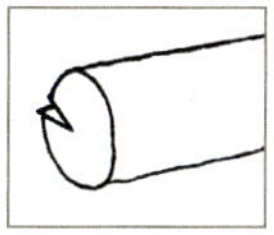

TYPE OF PROJECT House

SURFACE 689 feet^2 (210m^2)

LENGTH OF CONSTRUCTION 19 months

YEAR OF COMPLETION 2004

PHOTOS © Paul Ott

The team at Hertl Architekten was inspired by the majestic surroundings of the Lime National Park, in the Austrian Alps, to create this wooden house reminiscent of a forest shelter. The shaped logs make up a refined example of the romantic icon of the cabin. The legacy of vernacular houses such as the Irish turf houses are an inspiration for the project.

It is made up of two narrow houses, situated one next to the other, whose placement creates an open space that is used as a garden. It is an open, but protected, space from which fantastic views can be enjoyed: to the south is the valley and to the north the mountainside, which rises up above the building. The ground floor of the house is a single room, longer than it is wide, totally open to the outside, with

large windows that obscure the boundaries between the interior of the house and the natural surroundings. The appearance of the building meets the practical considerations of a rural area. The house adapts to the climate in a passive manner, through its structure; it is capable of creating a heat chamber between the walls, a good ventilation system, if the climatic conditions require it.

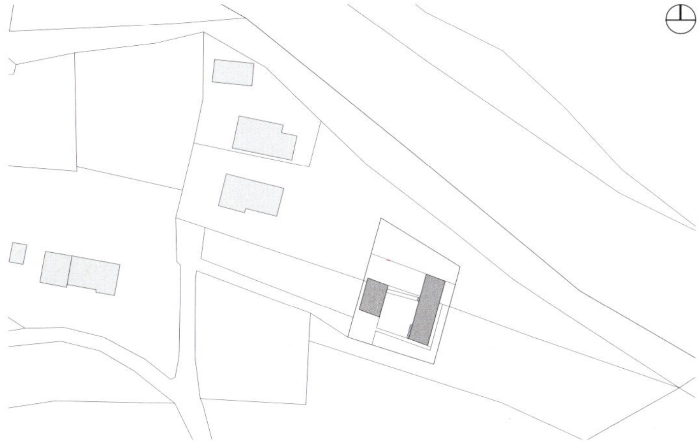

Site plan

The sensitivity of the material, the proportions of the house, and adaptation to the environment are fundamental basics in this project, which incorporates the virtues of wooden shelters from its predecessors. It also provides some practical improvements, such as the vast French windows which take full advantage of the light. The Seidl House constitutes an exercise in rational design that shows a series of interior and exterior spaces, which are reverently integrated into the surroundings.

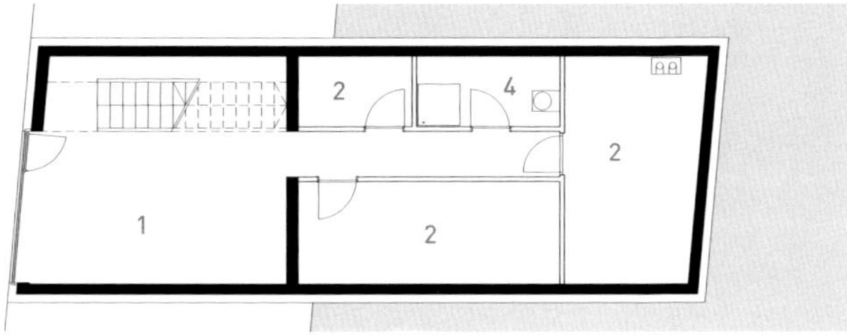

Basement

1 Studios
2 Storerooms

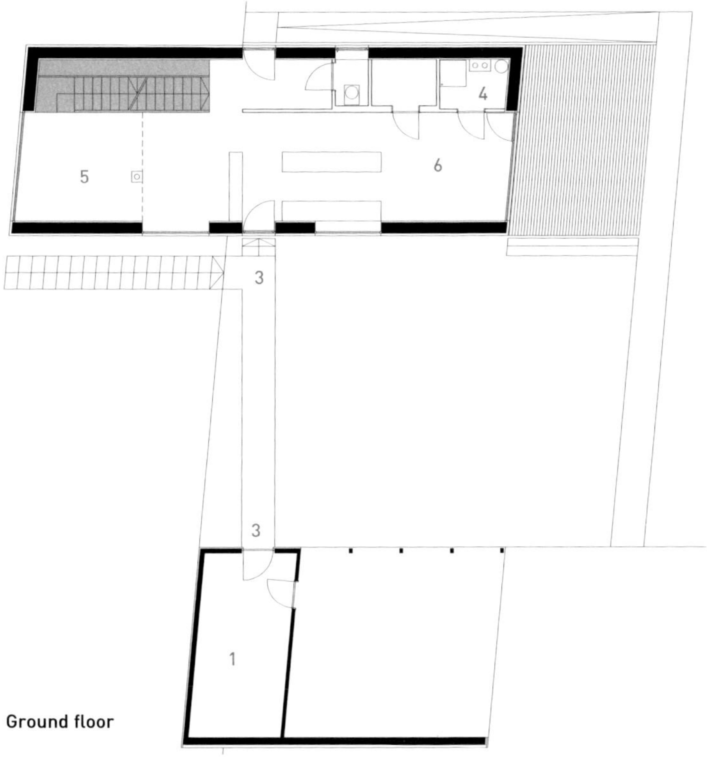

Ground floor

3 Entrances
4 Bathrooms
5 Lounge
6 Kitchen-diner

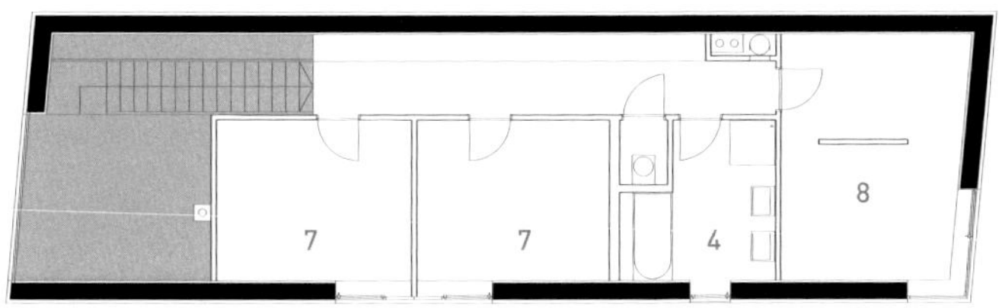

First floor

7 Bedrooms
8 Main bedroom

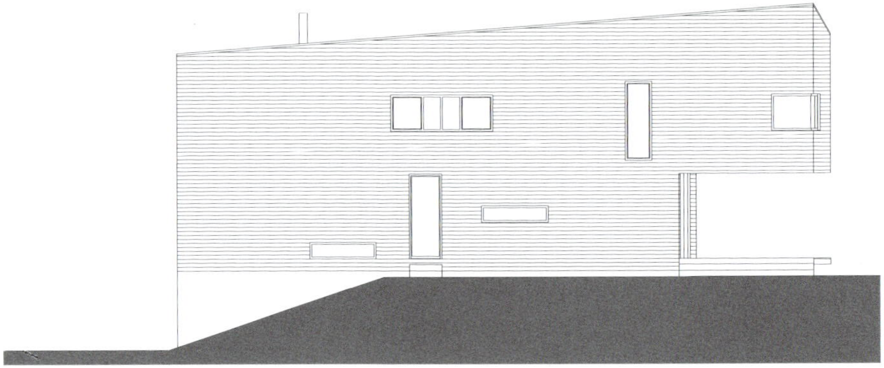

West elevation

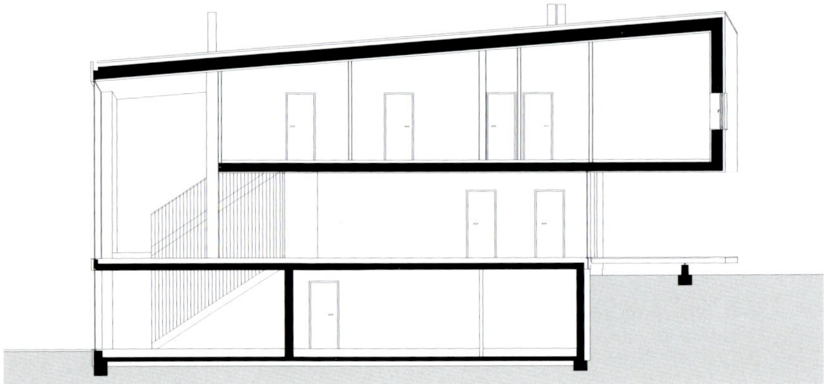

Longitudinal section

The openings to the outside, from enormous French windows to small windows that offer cut-outs of the landscape, become a design feature.

NEBESA MOUNTAIN RETREAT

AUTHOR Rok Klanjscek

LOCATION Livek, Kobarid, Slovenia

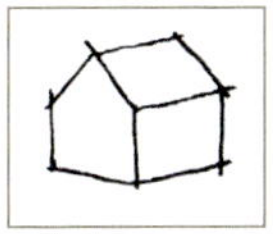 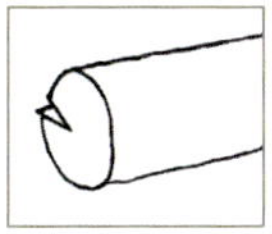

TYPE OF PROJECT Tourist resort

SURFACE 3,116.8 feet^2 (950m^2)

LENGTH OF CONSTRUCTION 24 months

YEAR OF COMPLETION 2004

PHOTOS © Miran Kambic

The Nebesa Mountain Retreat, situated in Livek, near Kobarid in Slovenia, is designed as a twenty-first century tourist complex. Rok Klanjscek designed a set of houses where traditional and modern meet and that imitate the surrounding mountains. The complex consists of a shelter from harsh weather, and at the same time, an impressive lookout surrounded by beautiful scenery.

Each of the houses has a unique perspective, which serves as a panoramic curtain, thanks to which extraordinary views can be seen. The large glass windows give the house a comfortable feeling and delineate a thin boundary between inside and outside. Situated in the tranquil surroundings of the protected area of Livek, this project brings together, from one side, respect for

tradition and local folklore, and, from the other, the latest advances in building techniques. Although the materials used are very similar to those used in the old cabins of the region, here they were put together in a more refined fashion, whilst still ensuring that the result was solid and long-lasting. Rok Klanjscek has used his observations of the century-old building of the area to find

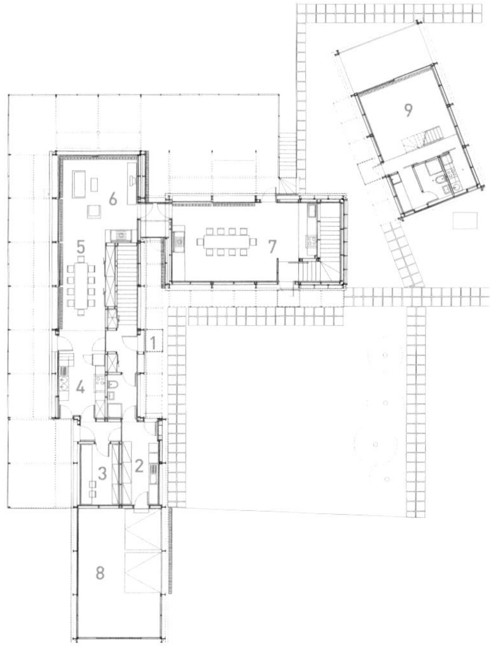

1 Entrance
2 Store room
3 Workshop
4 Kitchen
5 Dining room
6 Lounge
7 Meeting room
8 Parking space
9 Bungalow

Ground floor

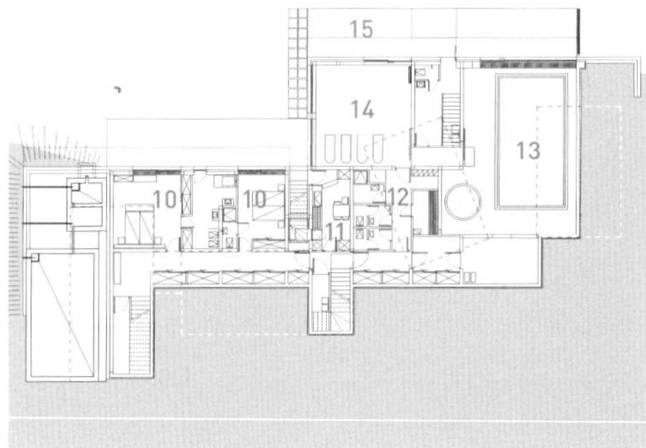

10 Bedrooms
11 Wine cellar
12 Spa area
13 Swimming pool
14 Gym
15 Terrace

Basement

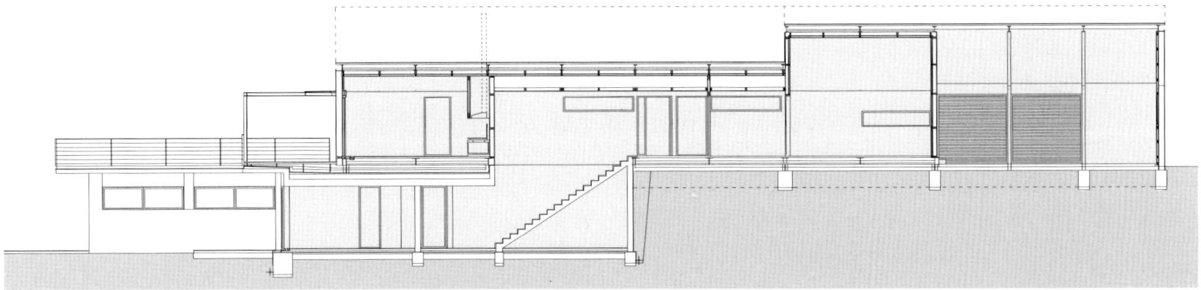

Longitudinal section

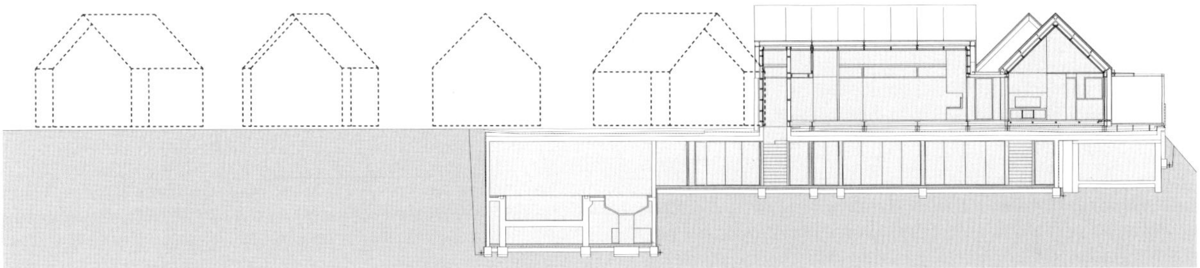

Cross section

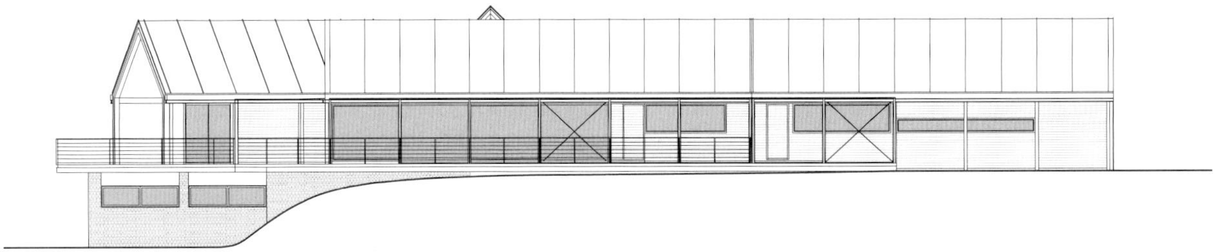

Side elevation

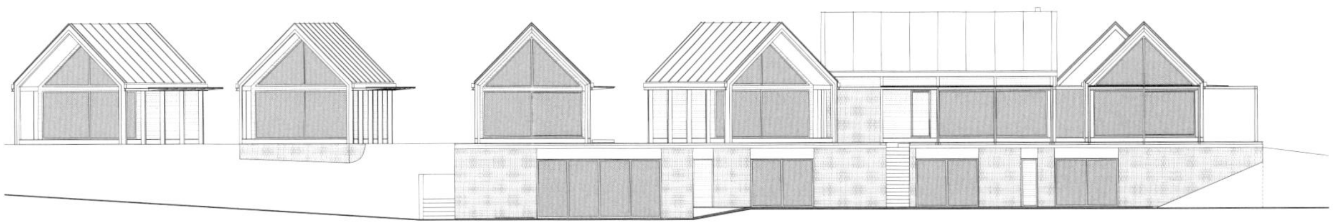

Front cross section

more practical solutions: stone and local wood continue to be the best and safest materials for the complex.

This complex of buildings has been created from all the knowledge passed down by local tradition, using a pure, clear, and simple architectural language. The complex recovers the cultural identity of the area and subtly blends into the environment with a design that is intentionally domestic in character. However, this is an exercise in contemporary architecture, which has put new building systems into practice that still use traditional long-lasting materials.

INTERVIEW WITH ROK KLANJSCEK

> THE HISTORICAL BUILDINGS OF THIS AREA WERE, FOR MANY CENTURIES, THE SAFEST, MOST PRACTICAL AND RATIONAL TYPE OF HOUSE FOR PEOPLE LIVING HERE.

Which ideas inspired this project?
Our projects, and especially those in the countryside, are inspired by local vernacular architecture. In this case, where the complex is situated in an isolated mountain region of Slovenia, we were inspired by the barns of the area and the typical character of an Alpine village.

How do you relate local vernacular architecture to your work?
We try to express the proportions of the design, urban density, architectural details, and local materials through a contemporary language that respects the regional traditions and architectural history of the place.

The inspiration from traditions and respect for them, thinking about the most typical examples and the use of local materials (in this case, stone, and wood) are, to my understanding, a prerequisite for successfully tackling the search for expressions of contemporary architecture.

NORDMARKA CABIN

AUTHOR Jarmund Vigsnæs Architects

LOCATION Nordmarka, Norway

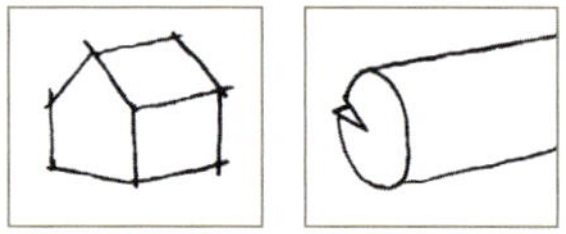

TYPE OF PROJECT House

SURFACE 393.7 feet^2 (120m^2)

LENGTH OF CONSTRUCTION 12 months

YEAR OF COMPLETION 2004

PHOTOS © Nils Petter

Situated in one of the few existing clearings in a dense Norwegian forest, the Nordmarka is carefully built in the hostile environment of the region. When planning this tranquil cabin, Jarmund Vigsnæs Architects studio made sure that it was facing the south, in the direction of a lake surrounded by rolling hills which continue on into the far away horizon.

The geometry of the building has been considered down to the last detail. The walls, the roof, and the frame of the building seem to have been shaped with the subtlety of a sculptor carving a piece of wood. The cabin is mainly lived in during the winter months, when there is a great deal of cross-country skiing in the surrounding woods. The architects designed

a two-storey building with a large central space in the middle, whose overhead light illuminates the side and upper areas of the building. The scale of the interior expands from small cubicles with beds to the main living area, which has a very high roof. Various additional spaces circle this central area and filter the natural light toward the heart of the cabin.

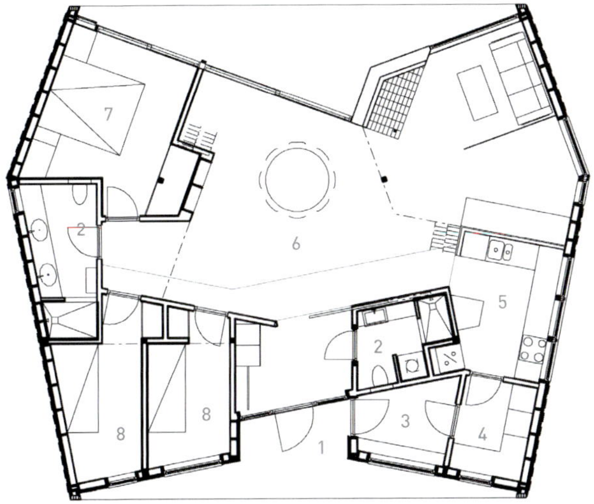

Ground floor

1 Entrance
2 Bathrooms
3 Store room
4 Pantry
5 Kitchen
6 Lounge-dining room
7 Main bedroom
8 Bedrooms
9 TV room
10 Machines

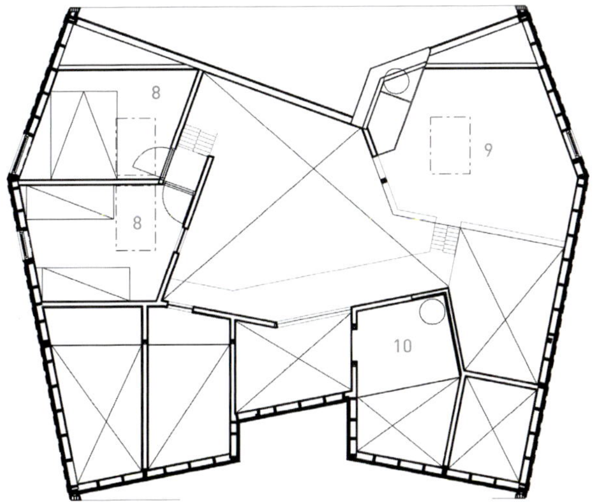

First floor

The building is set up to accommodate a number of guests. The relationship that exists between the small private spaces and the shared areas shows that the views from each one of them has been taken into accommodation.

With their selection of materials and colors, the Jarmund Vigsnæs Architects studio has followed the traditions of the region to the letter. The roof covering the house is made of dark treated wood, so that, in contrast, the interior is seen as a light-filled space, covered in untreated light-colored wood.

Despite its apparent simplicity, it can be said that the Nordmarka cabin is a robust building in which the additional areas insulate the heart of the retreat from the outside, as much in terms of space as light. This design recalls the structure of more sophisticated log houses, which had a compartmentalized space around a shared area where, next to the hearth, family life unfolded.

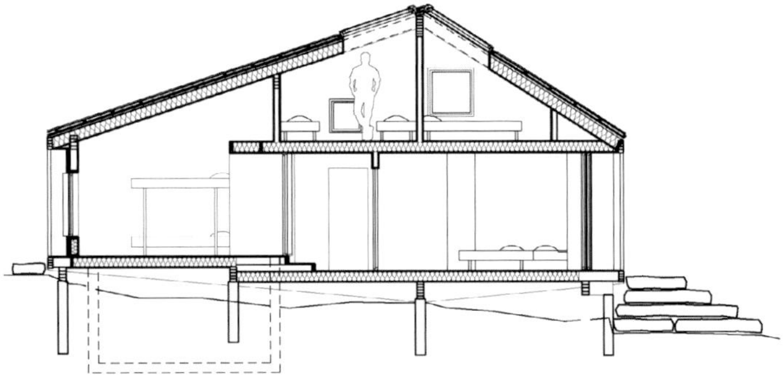

Cross section

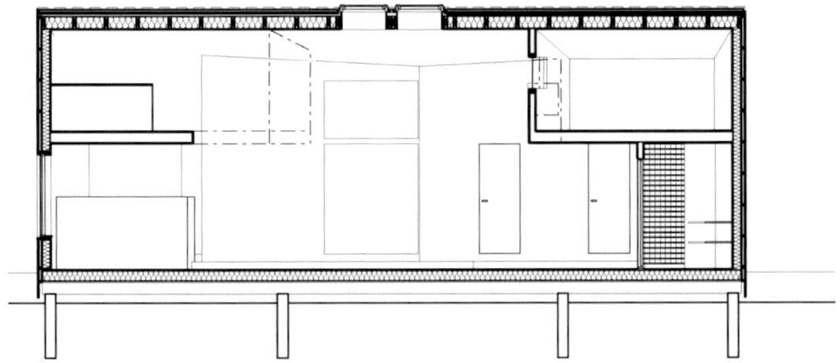

Longitudinal section

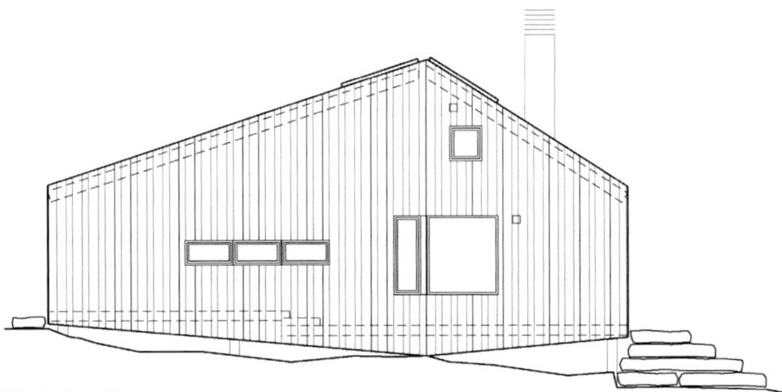

East elevation

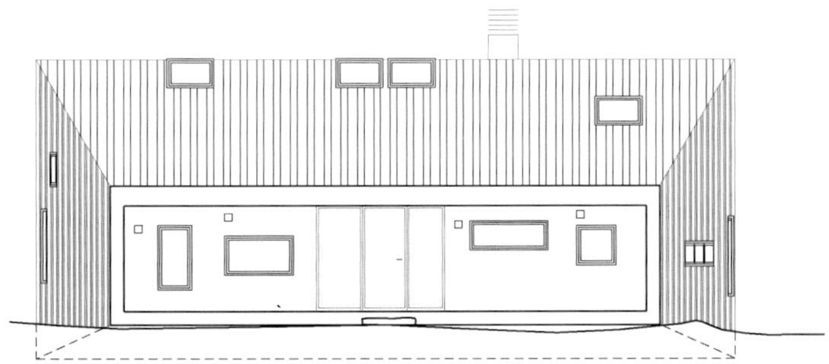

North elevation

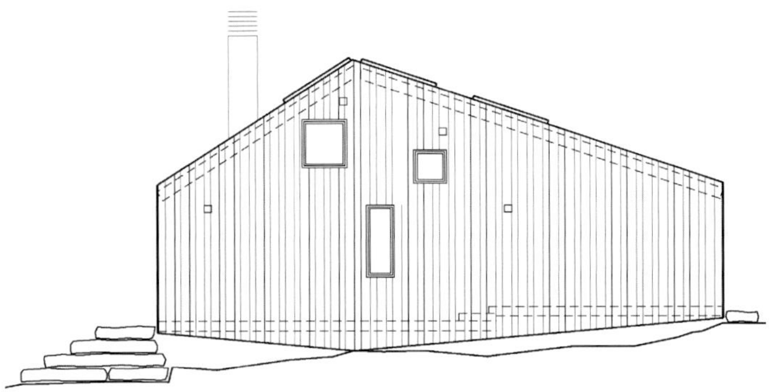

West elevation

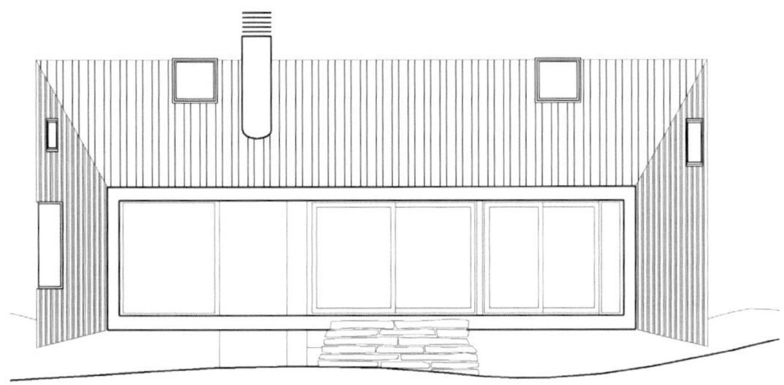

South elevation

HOUSE IN FLAWIL

AUTHOR Markus Wespi Jérôme de Meuron Architekten BSA

LOCATION Flawil, Switzerland

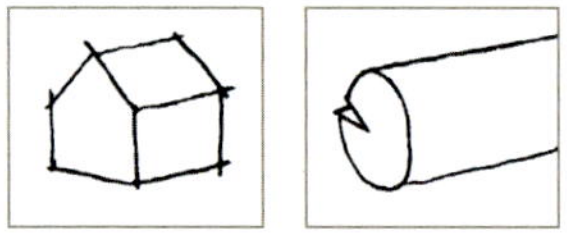

TYPE OF PROJECT House

SURFACE 459.3 feet^2 (140m^2)

LENGTH OF CONSTRUCTION 9 months

YEAR OF COMPLETION 2000

PHOTOS © Hannes Henz

The architects turned the remains of an old pre-fabricated wooden shed, in the agricultural area of Flawil in Switzerland, into a romantic countryside family house. The architects wanted, from an aesthetic point of view, their project to be in harmony with the rest of the cabins in the region; with this intention in mind, they tried to make the retreat seem as though it had always been there.

The old pre-fabricated building was very small and the only way of enlarging it was to extend it 4.9 feet (1.5m) on the south side. The architects of the project thought that the best option was to completely take out the south wall and replace it with windows, moving the building line as far as possible. On the other hand, the other three walls had no openings, an architectural decision applied

to the original structure, which turned out to be very useful for capturing solar energy in a passive manner. In the areas without windows, the wooden shingles form a compact and opaque surface. However, on the south side, only one in three shingles was installed so that the fields could be seen through the gaps. To keep the coherence of the composition, in the interior, wood is also used as a

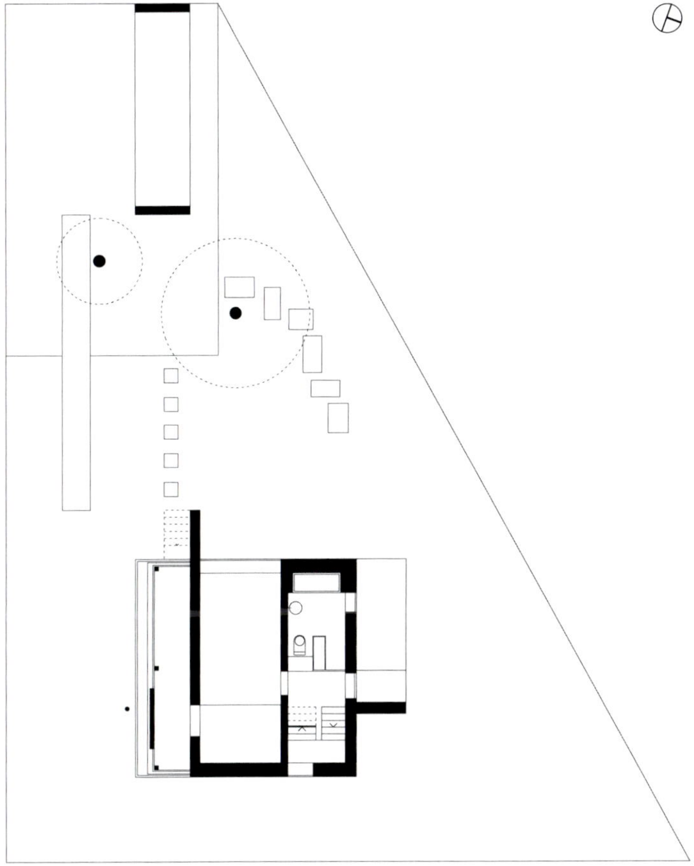

Site plan

building material. A small landscaped path leads up to the front doors of the house. The alternating sheets of wood are useful in two senses: they protect against the heat in the summer months, and keep the house private.

From far away, the country retreat seems to have no openings at all, giving it the appearance of a traditional barn of the area. The simplicity of its external structure and the use of wood as the basic building material are elements which rework the legacy of the first log houses from old Europe.

1 Entrance
2 Bathroom
3 Guest room
4 Gallery

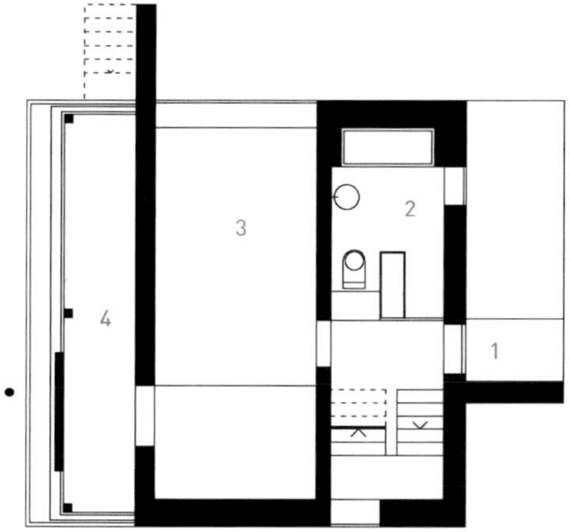

Ground floor

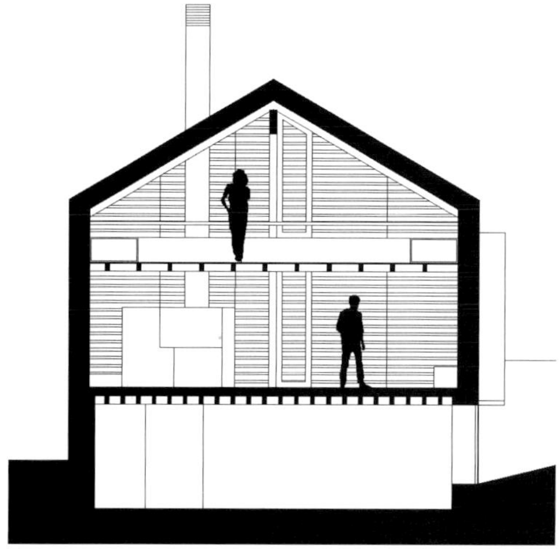

Cross section

5 Kitchen
6 Lounge

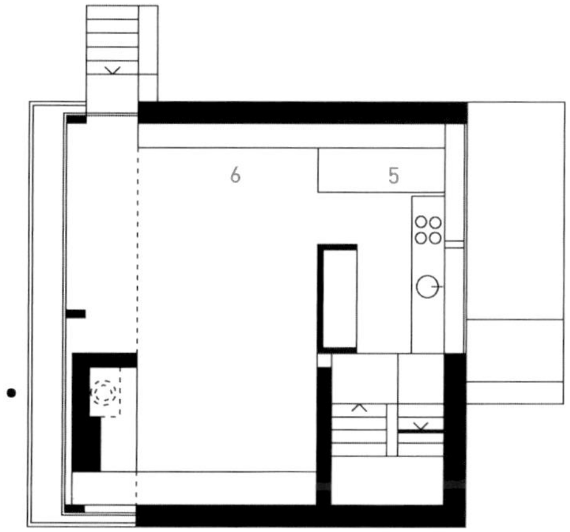

First floor

7 Study
8 Bedroom
9 Terrace

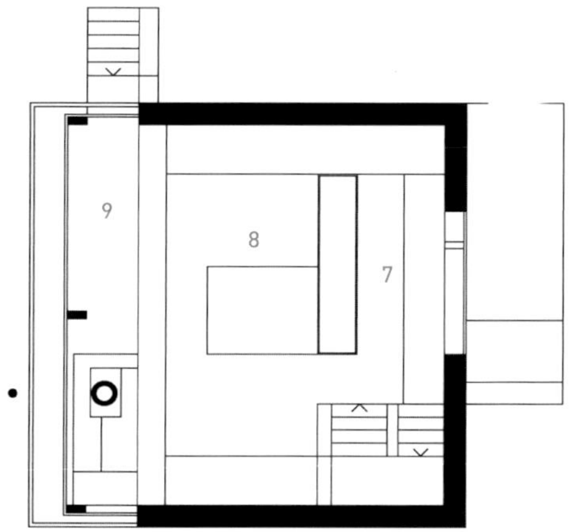

Second floor

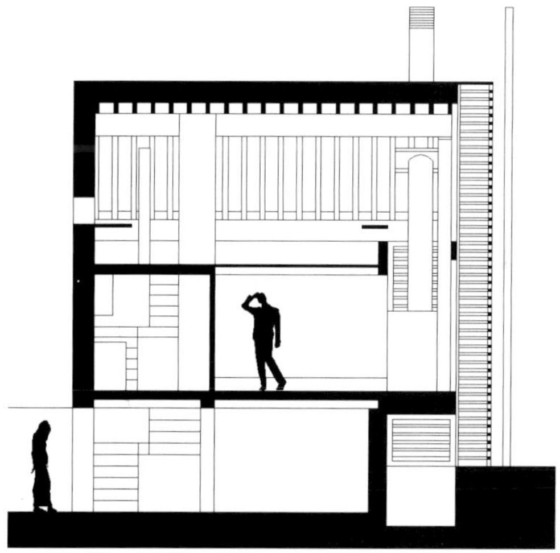

Longitudinal section

Although it has a hermetic, sealed appearance from outside, the gallery allows the surrounding countryside to be enjoyed.

INTERVIEW WITH MARKUS WESPI JÉRÔME DE MEURON ARCHITEKTE BSA

" NEW BUILDINGS SHOULD REFLECT THE TIME WHEN THEY WERE BUILT. "

What inspired you for the House in Flawil project?
We were thinking about the possibility of creating an indigenous and original project, on a smaller scale, which would bring the traditional barn to mind.

What importance does the observation of vernacular architecture have in your work?
We try to find where the qualities of the buildings are rooted or the environment of where they are, and we try to increase the possibilities with our interventions.

What can be learned from vernacular architecture?
We can learn a lot from vernacular architecture and the many features that each of its typologies offer. We think that the most important thing is to respect tradition, by trying not to fall into just producing copies without thinking.

Why do you believe that the cabin has become an icon of the vernacular house?
Probably because wood is a material which provides people with comfort and security.

SKI CHALET

AUTHOR EM2N

LOCATION Cafrida, Flumserberg-Tannenheim, Switzerland

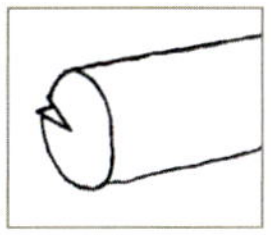

TYPE OF PROJECT House

SURFACE 341.2 feet^2 (104m^2)

LENGTH OF CONSTRUCTION 12 months

YEAR OF COMPLETION 2003

PHOTOS © Hannes Henz

Most mountain chalets in the Swiss Alps look the same, but the architects of EM2N wanted to move away from the archetypal model of houses in this area. They, therefore, planned a building that was not at all conventional, situated on the ski slopes of Cafrida in Flumserberg.

The chalet is different from the neighboring houses, due to the vertical shape of the building, which gives a privileged position over the surroundings without interfering in the environment. The house's garden is simply nature itself, without borders, with its own meandering path leading out into the wilderness. This futuristic cabin with panoramic views over the valley more closely resembles a house belonging to a business executive than to a large family. The

structure of the retreat is the antithesis of a compartmentalized house. There are no closed rooms, only vertical and horizontal areas that correspond to the various necessary functions. The beauty of the project does not lie so much in the details and the quality of the materials used as in the placement and distribution of the available space. The architects of EM2N tried to break with

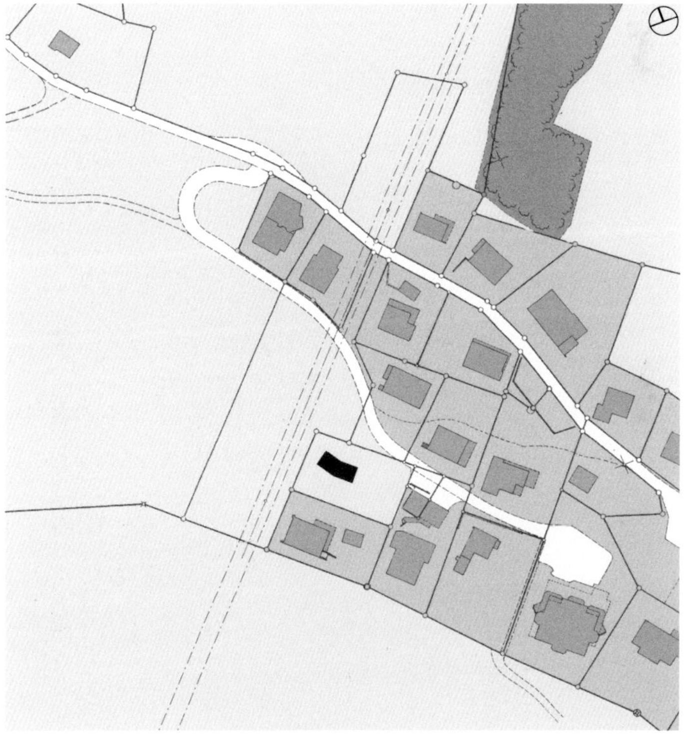

Site plan

the classic Alpine cliché of a dark wood cabin with small windows like those found in pre-fabricated models. With a singular effort at innovation, their building reinterprets the legacy of the log house through a new expression, modern and unique, that is far from current stereotypes.

The sophisticated finishing of the project plays with the form, materials, and proportions of the classic Swiss cabin in a way which is almost ironic. The resulting building makes full use of the privileged site of the plot, highlights the value of the topography, and integrates harmoniously into the surroundings.

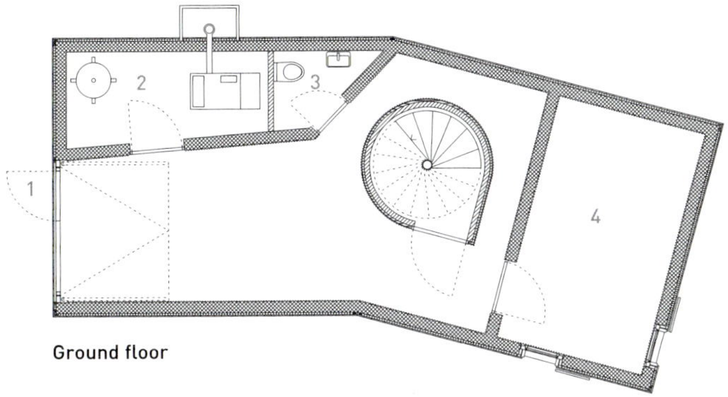

Ground floor

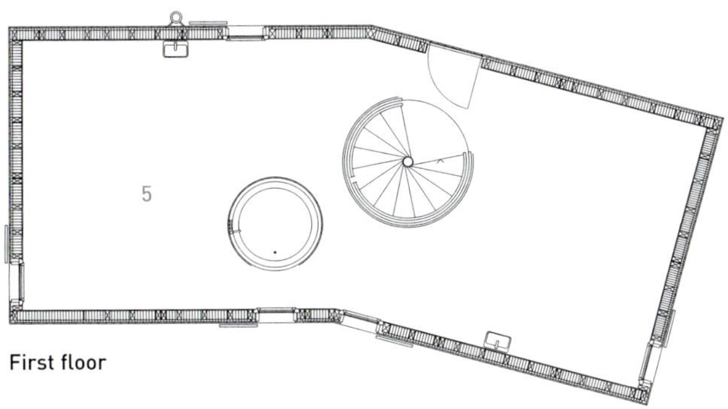

First floor

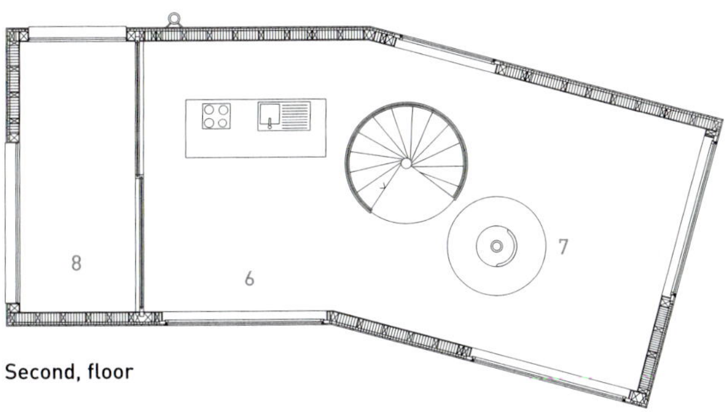

Second, floor

1 Entrance
2 Kitchen-diner
3 Washroom
4 Bedroom
5 Bathroom-sleeping area
6 Kitchen-diner
7 Lounge
8 Terrace

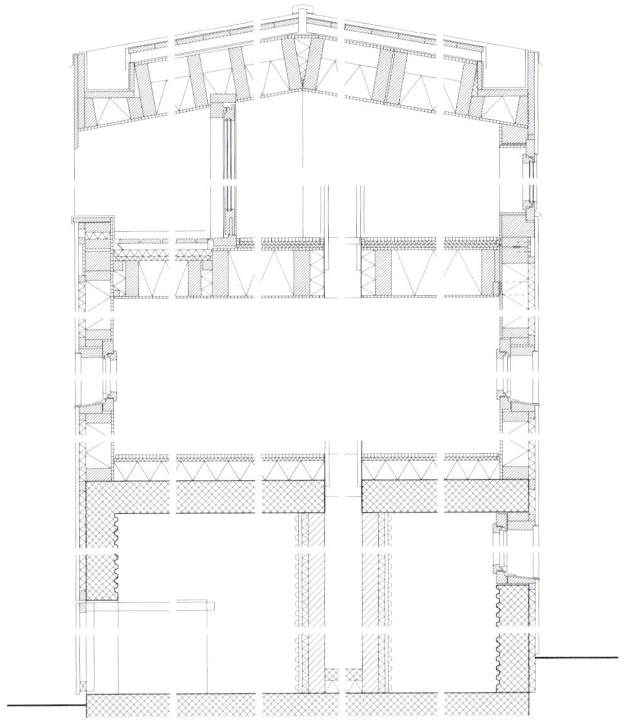

Building cross section

The details and finishing of the cabin highlight the rustic character of the small building and reveal the building process.

“FROM VERNACULAR ARCHITECTURE, WE MUST RETAIN SIMPLICITY WITHOUT FALLING INTO THE TRAP OF BEING SIMPLE, ATTRACTIVE WITHOUT BECOMING TOO RECOGNIZABLE, TRADITIONAL WITHOUT BECOMING KITSCH.”

Did you take the cabin into account as inspiration for this ski chalet?
In Switzerland, the idea of the traditional wood cabin does not exist. Instead, we find other typical typologies, such as the farm and traditional Alpine hut, most of which are made of pieces of wood, or stone, or both materials together. With the arrival of the first tourist complexes in the twentieth century, forms of traditional lodgings were gradually disappearing and gave way to a generic "Alpine" architecture.
We are interested in working with local cultural conventions, which in this case are not lost local traditions, but rather the cliché of the Swiss-Austrian Alpine chalet. From there, we play around in an ironic manner with the formulas of this typology to change the form, proportions, details, and spaces inside the house.

What importance does the observation of vernacular architecture have in your work?
We are interested in the basic qualities of vernacular architecture, such as the relationship it has with the site or the rawness it shows. However, we do not believe in retrospective architecture that recreates forgotten styles and tends to make us think that we are living in another century. Our architecture has its place today and we must look for its roots in our reality.

Why do you believe that the cabin has become an icon which is so closely linked to the home?
The "Heidi syndrome" could explain part of this point of view. The cabin and the Alpine chalet have become clichés which make us dream of a simple life and living at one with nature. In the context of a globalized culture like ours, we find it difficult to embrace these clichés, and instead, we prefer to destroy them by using irony. Our chalet aimed to fulfill the James Bond fantasy as much as the Heidi cliché.

IMAGE AND PHOTO CREDITS

Pages 3-23
Maps and illustrations:
Montse Montero

Photos:
Fred Hultstrand Collection, NDIRS-NDSU, Fargo. North Dakota State University Institute for Regional Studies; page 6.

U.S. Library of Congress, Prints and Photographs Division, Historic American Buildings Survey or Historic American Engineering Record; pages 8, 9, 10, 11 (left), 12 (right), 13, 14, 16, 17, 21, 22, 23.

Taken by Maureen Jameson in Nashville, Tennessee, January 1 2005. Published under a Creative Commons license. http://creativecommons.org/licenses/by/3.0/; page 15.

National Anthropological Archives, Smithsonian Institution, GN 01000b; page 12 (left).

Pages 24-139
Photos credited on each project.

BIBLIOGRAPHY

Boericke, Art; Shapiro, Barry
Maisons de charpentiers amateurs américains
Chêne
1976

Boericke, Art; Shapiro, Barry
Maisons faites à la maison
Chêne/Hachette
1979

Hunt, Ben
How to Build and Furnish a Log Cabin
Wiley
1974

Miller, Judith
Casas De Madera
Blume
1998

Oliver, Paul
Dwellings: The Vernacular House World Wide
Phaidon
2003

Shasmoukine, Annie; Shasmoukine, Pierre
Construire en bois
Alternative et Parallèles
1980

Slavid, Ruth
Arquitectura En Madera
Blume
2005

Upton, Dell
Common Places: Readings in American Vernacular Architecture
University of Georgia Press
1986

Weslager, C. A.
The Log Cabin in America
Rutgers University Press
1969

WEBOGRAPHY

Digital library of the Appalachians:
www.aca-dla.org/site-templates/logessay.html

The United States Department of National Parks:
www.nps.gov

American studies of the University of Virginia:
xroads.virginia.edu/~UG97/albion/acabin.html

Camp Silos organization:
www.campsilos.org/mod2/teachers/r3_part2.shtm

International Information Programs of the United States:
usinfo.state.gov/products/pubs/histryotln/expansion.htm

DIRECTORY

3RW Architects
PB 1131
5809 Bergen, Norway
T: +47 55 36 55 36
F: +47 55 36 55 37
3rw@3rw.no
www.3rw.no

Bakker & Blanc Architectes
Rue des Terreaux 5
1003 Lucerne, Switzerland
T: +41 21 311 95 27
F: +41 21 311 95 28
info@bakkerblanc.ch
www.bakkerblanc.ch

Broadhurst Architects
306 First Street
Rockville, MD 20851, United States
T: +1 301 309 8900
F: +1 301 309 8915
jbroadhurst@broadhurstarchitects.com
www.broadhurstarchitects.com

BURO II bvba / BURO Interior bvba
Hoogleedsesteenweg 415
8800 Roeselare, Belgium
T: +32 51 21 11 05
F: +32 51 22 46 74
info@buro2.be
www.buro2.be

El Dorado
510 César E. Chávez Avenue
Kansas City, MO 64108, United States
T: +1 816 474 3838
F: +1 816 474 0836
nwoodfill@eldoradoarchitects.com
www.eldoradoarchitects.com

EM2N
Josefstrasse 92
8005 Zurich, Switzerland
T: +41 44 215 60 10
F: +41 44 215 60 11
em2n@em2n.ch
www.em2n.ch

Felipe Assadi
Carmencita 262, of. 202
Las Condes, Santiago 7550056, Chile
T: +56 2 234 5558
info@assadi.cl
www.felipeassadi.com

Hertl Architekten
Zwischenbrücken 4
A-4400 Steyr, Austria
T: +43 7252 46944
F: +43 7252 47363
steyr@hertl-architekten.com
www.hertl-architekten.com

Jarmund Vigsnæs Architects
Hausmannsgate 6
0186 Oslo, Norway
T: +47 22 99 43 43
F: +47 22 99 43 53
jva@jva.no
www.jva.no

Markus Wespi Jérôme de Meuron Architekten BSA
Keine Strassenbezeichnung
6578 Caviano, Switzerland
T: +41 91 794 17 73
F: +41 91 794 17 73
info@wespidemeuron.ch
www.wespidemeuron.ch

Rok Klanjscek
Tovarniska 17
1000 Ljubljana, Slovenia
T: +386 41 773139
F: +386 1 5852672
rok.klanjscek@real-eng.si

Taylor_Smyth Architects
354 Davenport Road, Suite 3B
Toronto, ON M5R 1K6, Canada
T: +1 416 968 6688
F: +1 416 968 7728
info@taylorsmyth.com
www.taylorsmyth.com

Verdickt & Verdickt Architecten
Oranjestraat 44
2060 Amberes, Belgium
T: +32 3 233 83 51
F: +32 3 233 83 52
info@verdicktenverdickt.be
www.verdicktenverdickt.be

Vidal & Sant'Anna Arquitetura
José Eusebio 95, casa 110
01239 030 São Paulo, Brazil
T: +55 11 3214 6102
F: +55 11 3256 2977
vsarquitetura@vsarquitetura.com.br
www.vsarquitetura.com.br

Schiffer